THE AMERICAN LAW RELATING TO INCOME AND PRINCIPAL

Published @ 2017 Trieste Publishing Pty Ltd

ISBN 9780649473984

The American Law Relating to Income and Principal by Edwin A. Howes

Except for use in any review, the reproduction or utilisation of this work in whole or in part in any form by any electronic, mechanical or other means, now known or hereafter invented, including xerography, photocopying and recording, or in any information storage or retrieval system, is forbidden without the permission of the publisher, Trieste Publishing Pty Ltd, PO Box 1576 Collingwood, Victoria 3066 Australia.

All rights reserved.

Edited by Trieste Publishing Pty Ltd.
Cover @ 2017

This book is sold subject to the condition that it shall not, by way of trade or otherwise, be lent, re-sold, hired out, or otherwise circulated without the publisher's prior consent in any form or binding or cover other than that in which it is published and without a similar condition including this condition being imposed on the subsequent purchaser.

www.triestepublishing.com

EDWIN A. HOWES

THE AMERICAN LAW RELATING TO INCOME AND PRINCIPAL

Trieste

THE AMERICAN LAW

RELATING TO

INCOME AND PRINCIPAL

BY

EDWIN A. HOWES, JR.

A.B., LL.B., HARV.

OF THE SUFFOLK BAR

BOSTON

LITTLE, BROWN, AND COMPANY

1905

Econ 7422.70

Mrs. Robert F. Raymond

Copyright, 1905,
By Edwin A. Howes, Jr.

All rights reserved

THE UNIVERSITY PRESS, CAMBRIDGE, U.S.A.

PREFACE.

THIS book is the result of an attempt to present in concise and convenient form, and to explain, the various rules of law applicable to the separation of the returns from investments into what is properly income and what should be held as principal. Although the subject is largely a branch of the law of trusts, no book on trusts has given it the detailed attention that its importance deserves. On disputed points of law a full citation of authorities has been given, with the purpose of indicating the law in each state; but for the most part only such cases have been cited as seemed necessary to illustrate the principles which they support.

It is hoped that the book will prove useful, not only to lawyers, but to trustees and accountants, and the book has been designed for such general use.

EDWIN A. HOWES, JR.

OCTOBER 2, 1905.

CONTENTS.

	PAGE
TABLE OF CASES	xv

CHAPTER I.

INTRODUCTION	1
Definition of income and of principal	1
Real income distinguished from apparent income	1

CHAPTER II.

WASTING INVESTMENTS	4
Income must not consume principal	4
Leasehold estates	5
Mines, quarries, oil wells	5
"Open" mines	5
Intention of creator of estate prevails	6
Timber	7
Not entirely income	7
Estovers or botes	7
English law as to profit in woodland	8
American law as to profit in woodland	9
Trees cut for purpose of clearing	10
Trees blown down	11
Trees cut in manner customary on estate	12
Intention of creator of estate prevails	12
Bonds bought at a premium	13
Premium to be made up, how	13
Intention of creator, effect of	15

CONTENTS.

	PAGE
Bonds forming part of original property	16
No sinking fund in case of	16
Profit on sale of bonds belongs to principal	16

CHAPTER III.

DIVIDENDS ON SHARES OF STOCK	17
Dividends must not waste principal	17
Income of corporation not income of stockholder until declaration of dividend	17
Discretion of directors when to declare dividends	17
Dividends presumed to be from income	18
Regular dividends	18
Safe to treat as from earnings unless stated to be otherwise	18
Owner of stock at time dividend declared, entitled to whole	19
Wasting dividends belong partly to principal	19
Effect of intention of creator of estate as to	19
Extraordinary cash dividends	20
Not usually based upon current earnings	20
Accumulation of undivided earnings increases value of stock	20
Apportionment of, between principal and income	21
Massachusetts rule against apportionment	22
Pennsylvania rule in favor of apportionment	23
Criticisms of both rules	24
Stock dividends	25
Nature of	25
Massachusetts rule that they belong to principal	26
Pennsylvania rule that they be treated the same as cash dividends	28

CONTENTS.

	PAGE
When apportioned	28
Method of apportionment	29
New York rule	30
Option to take cash or stock	31
Treated as cash dividend, when	31
Treated as stock dividend, when	32
Division of old stock bought by the company	33
Income if bought with earnings	33
When principal	33
Dividend in form of bonds issued by the company, similar to stock dividend	33
Delayed dividends distinguished from extraordinary dividends	33
Dividends out of capital of corporation	34
Meaning of word capital	34
Fundamental capital	34
Working capital	35
Floating capital	35
Dividends from fundamental capital belong to principal	35
Value of property remaining is immaterial	36
Cases of mergers	36
Dividends out of profit due to increase in value of fundamental capital are principal	37
Dividends by land companies based on increase belong to income	38
Dividends from capitalized earnings belong to principal	39
Dividends from floating capital are dividends from income	39
Dividends from proceeds of working capital purchased with earnings	41
On principle, should be treated as from income	42

CONTENTS.

	PAGE
Position of courts doubtful	45
Dividends in liquidation	45
In Massachusetts and Connecticut belong entirely to principal	45
Rule in New York different	46
Rights belong to principal	46
They are not dividends	46
Summary of chapter	47

CHAPTER IV.

APPORTIONMENT OF LOSS OR PROFIT BETWEEN PRINCIPAL AND INCOME	50
Loss of principal not made up from income	50
Loss of income not made up from principal	50
Partial loss to both, how apportioned	50
On foreclosure of mortgage	50
On devastavit by trustee	53
Profit on foreclosure proceedings apportioned on same principle	52

CHAPTER V.

WHEN ENJOYMENT OF INCOME BEGINS	54
Enjoyment of annuity or income given by will begins at death of testator	54
Different intention of testator given effect	54
Income in case of delayed conversion	55
Beneficiary entitled to equitable income	55
Actual income greater than equitable	55
Actual income less than equitable	56
Method of determining equitable income	56
Situations where doctrine is applied	57
Investments in shipping, partnership, leaseholds, vacant land	57
Doctrine modified by testator's intention	58

CONTENTS. xi

	PAGE
Accumulated income	59
Belongs to principal if no direction to pay out as income	59
Temporarily withheld belongs to income	59

CHAPTER VI.

	PAGE
OUTLAY	60
Corpus to be kept intact	60
Taxes	60
Ordinary taxes to be paid from income	60
Water rates to be paid from income	60
Ordinary taxes not usually apportioned as to time	61
Taxes for permanent improvements	61
Apportioned between life-tenant and remainderman	61
In case of trust estate, paid out of principal	62
Taxes for lasting improvements	62
Paid from income if improvements are likely to wear out during life estate	62
If likely to last longer, apportioned between corpus and income according to benefit received by each	62
Taxes on unproductive property paid from principal	63
Inheritance tax paid from estate or interest taxed	63
Repairs	64
Ordinary repairs paid from income	64
Additions and alterations paid from principal	64
On newly purchased property, paid from principal	65
Trustee's judgment in apportioning expense of repairs and improvements not disturbed unless clearly wrong	65

	PAGE
Insurance	66
Life tenant not bound to insure	66
Trustee bound to insure whole estate	66
Expense payable from income	66
Insurance money on whole estate is principal	66
Incumbrances	66
Interest on, paid from income	66
Principal of, if paid by trustee comes out of corpus	67
If principal of is paid by remainderman, life tenant must continue to pay interest	67
Expenses of management of estate paid from income	67
Trustee's charges for services	67
Trustee's commissions for collection of principal	68
Brokerage on changes of investment	68
Brokerage on purchase or sale of real estate charged to principal	68
Costs and expenses of bill for instructions payable from principal	69
Expenses of administration payable from principal	69

CHAPTER VII.

APPORTIONMENT OF CURRENT INCOME AS TO TIME	70
General principle	70
Rent not apportionable by common law	70
Rent, to what extent apportionable by statute	71
Annuities	73
Definition of	73
Not apportionable by common law	73
Exceptions to general rule	73
Annuities for support	73
Annuities in lieu of dower	73
To what extent apportionable by statute	74
Payable when	74

	PAGE
Dividends, regular	74
Not apportioned	74
Effect of apportionment statutes	75
Declared before but paid after death of life tenant, are income	76
By savings banks are not apportioned	77
Profits of business not apportioned	76
Interest	77
On debts and loans apportioned	77
On mortgage notes apportioned	78
On public debt not apportioned	78
On coupon bonds	78
Not apportioned in some States	78
Apportioned in other States	79

CHAPTER VIII.

A SUMMARY OF THE STATUTES AND DECISIONS IN THE VARIOUS STATES BEARING UPON APPORTIONMENT OF CURRENT INCOME ... 80

Arkansas	80
Connecticut	80
Delaware	80
Georgia	81
Illinois	81
Indiana	81
Indian Territory	81
Iowa	82
Kentucky	82
Massachusetts	82
Michigan	84
Mississippi	84
Missouri	85
New Hampshire	85
New Jersey	85

	PAGE
New York	85
North Carolina	87
Ohio	87
Pennsylvania	87
Rhode Island	88
South Carolina	88
Tennessee	89
Virginia	89
West Virginia	89
Wisconsin	89
INDEX	93

TABLE OF CASES CITED.

	PAGE
ABELL v. Brady	64
Adams v. Adams	23, 27, 71, 75, 83
Allis' Estate, In re	13
Armitage, In re	23, 46
Armstrong v. Wilson	8
Ashhurst v. Field's Adm'r	29
Atkins v. Albree	46
Ayer v. Ayer	54
BABCOCK, Matter of	61
Bailey's Estate	73, 88
Balch v. Hallet	5, 39
Banner v. Lowe	78
Bartlett, Petitioner	69
Bateman v. Hotchkin (No. 2)	11
Bates v. Barry	73
Bates v. Mackinley	25, 77
Bedford's Appeal	7, 13
Biddell's Appeal	46
Blakley v. Marshall	5
Blight v. Blight	74, 88
Bobb v. Wolff	62
Borie v. Crissman	72
Bouch v. Sproule	27, 33, 45
Bowditch v. Soltyk	69
Bradley v. Bailey	80
Bradley's Estate	63
Bridge v. Bridge	60, 66
Brinley v. Grou	46
Browne v. Collins	76
Brown v. Gellatly	57
Brown and Larned, Petitioners	27
Brown v. Wright	59
Brown's Estate	64
Buckingham v. Morrison	58
Bulkeley v. Stephens	77
Burt v. Gill	59
Butterbaugh's Appeal	67
CAIRNS v. Chabert	60
Caldecott v. Brown	64
Chase v. Darby	73, 74, 84
Clapp v. Astor	70, 75, 86
Clark v. Holden	10
v. Middlesworth	63
Clemence v. Steere	11, 64
Clifford v. Davis	54
Clyburn v. Reynolds	66
Cobb v. Fant	24, 29
Connolly's Estate (No. 1)	24
Cook v. Lowry	53
Crump's Estate	61
Cushing v. Burrell	54
Cushing's Will, In re	73
DALAND v. Williams	26, 33
Danly v. Cummins's Ex'r	68
Dashwood v. Magniac	8, 12
Davis v. Jackson	18, 25, 31
Deane v. Home for Aged Colored Women	69
De Koven v. Alsop	23, 27, 46
De Witt v. Cooper	60, 66
Dexter v. Phillips	70, 71, 78, 79, 84
D'Ooge v. Leeds	26, 33
Drown v. Smith	10
Dufford v. Smith	60

TABLE OF CASES CITED.

	PAGE
EARP'S APPEAL	24, 29, 30
Earp's Will	79
Edwards v. Edwards	56, 57
Eichelberger's Estate	54
Eisner's Appeal	47
Eley's Appeal	6, 7, 18
FINDLAY v. Smith	12
Fleet v. Dorland	62
Flickwir's Estate	54
Foote, Appellant	75, 84
Franklin, Matter of	72, 86
GERRY, Matter of	16
Gheen v. Osborn	88
Gibbons v. Mahon	18, 20, 23, 27, 28
Gibson v. Bott	74
Gifford v. Thompson	21, 23, 46
Gilkey v. Paine	33
Gordon v. West	68
Graham's Estate	16
Granger v. Bassett	75, 83
Green v. Crapo	58
Greene v. Huntington	75, 77, 80
v. Smith	27, 46
HAGAN v. Platt	52
v. Varney	60
Harrison v. Pepper	66
Harrison's Trust, In re	8, 11
Healey v. Toppan	55, 57
Heard v. Eldredge	17, 35, 86, 68
Heighe v. Littig	58
Heizer v. Heizer	73
Hemenway v. Hemenway	14, 23, 39, 40, 41, 45, 46, 84
Henry v. Henderson	73, 74
Hill v. Newichawanick Co.	76, 86
Hite's Devisees v. Hite's Ex'r	15, 23, 31, 46, 58
Hitner v. Ege	62, 63
Holmes v. Taber	60, 61
Honywood v. Honywood	8, 9
Hoyt, Matter of	16
Hubbuck, In re	52
Huff v. Latimer	88

	PAGE
Huston v. Tribbetts	62
Hyatt v. Allen	75, 86
JOHNSON, Matter of	13
v. Bridgewater, etc., Co.	77
v. Johnson	10, 11
Jones v. Ogle	76
KANE, Matter of	86
Kearney v. Cruikshank	73, 74
v. Ex'r of Kearney	64
Keeler v. Eastman	10
Keith v. Copeland	55
Kernochan, Matter of	20, 21, 23, 71, 86
King v. Miller	10
Kinmonth v. Brigham	55, 57
Koen v. Bartlett	
LACKAWANNA Iron and Coal Co., In re	73, 85
Lang's Ex'r v. Lang	24, 29
Leland v. Hayden	33, 41
Lester v. Young	11
Little v. Little	64, 65
Lord Londesborough v. Somerville	77
Lord v. Brooks	29
Lovering v. Minot	54
Lowry v. Farmers' Loan & Tr. Co.	31
Lyman v. Pratt	31
MALAM, In re	31
Mann v. Anderson	75
Marshall v. Moseley	86
Martens' Estate, In re	63
Martin v. Martin	67
McClintock v. Dana	6, 7
McCullough v. Irvine's Ex'rs	10
McKeen's Appeal	71, 76, 88
McLouth v. Hunt	31
Meldon v. Devlin	52
Meldrin v. Trustees of Trinity Church	33
Mercer v. Buchanan	35, 86, 88
Millen v. Guerrard	23, 31
Miller, Estate of	62

TABLE OF CASES CITED. xvii

	PAGE
Miller v. Crawford	72, 86
Mills, Adm'r v. Britton	33
Minot v. Paine	17, 23, 26, 40
v. Tappan	59
v. Thompson	5, 55, 57
Modlin v. Kennedy	10, 11
Moore v. Simonson	61, 67
Morehouse v. Cotheal	11
Moss's Appeal	46, 47
Mower v. Sandford	74, 80
Mudge v. Parker	55, 57
Murch v. Smith M'f'g Co.	63, 64
NEEL'S Estate	53
Nehls v. Sauer	73, 82
New England Trust Co. v. Eaton	13, 14, 15
N. Y. Life Ins. & Tr. Co. v. Baker	13
Noble v. Tyler	87
Noyes v. Stone	8
OLIVER'S Estate	39
Outcalt v. Appleby	58
Owen v. Hyde	10
PARKER v. Ames	68, 69
v. Hill	68
v. Seeley	52, 74, 85
Park's Estate	16, 52
Parr, In re	64
Parsons v. Winslow	52, 53, 65
Patterson v. Johnson	68
Pearly v. Smith	78
Peck v. Sherwood	62
Peirce v. Burroughs	29, 46, 60, 67
Penn-Gaskell's Estate (No. 2)	15
Perry v. Aldrich	85
Pitcairn, In re	58
Plympton v. Boston Dispensary	60, 62, 63, 67
Pratt v. Douglas	62, 64
Pritchitt v. Nashville Tr. Co.	24, 29
Proctor, Matter of	16
QUINN v. Madigan	69, 73, 85
v. Safe Dep. & Tr. Co.	25, 40

	PAGE
RAND v. Hubbell	18, 20, 22, 23, 27, 33
Redmon v. Bedford	72, 82
Reed v. Head	16, 19
Reyburn v. Wallace	62, 63
R. I. Hospital Tr. Co. v. Harris	74
Richardson v. Richardson	23, 27
Ridge, In re	5, 7
Riggs v. Cragg	78, 86
Rogers, Matter of	36, 40, 41, 46
Ross's Estate	75, 88
Rowan v. Riley	72, 89
Rutledge, Ex parte	75
SARGENT v. Sargent	16, 54, 83, 84
Sayers v. Hoskinson	10
Second Un. Ch. v. Colegrove	21, 23, 27, 40, 46
Shaw v. Cordis	16
Shoemaker's Appeal	6
Smith v. Dana	18, 39, 42
v. Fellows	54
v. Hooper	37, 88
v. Smith	10, 11
Smith's Estate	24, 29
Sohier v. Eldridge	64, 65, 70
Spangler's Estate	68
Spencer v. Scurr	6
Spooner v. Phillips	27
Stewart v. Phelps	41
Stone v. Littlefield	52, 63
Stonebraker v. Zollickoffer	10, 11
THOMAS v. Gregg	24, 29, 30
Thomson's Estate	39, 47
Tracy, Matter of	60
Tragbar's Estate	63
Trenton Tr. etc. Co. v. Donnelly	51, 58
Tuttle's Case	52
U. S. Trust Co. v. Tobias	79, 87
VAN DOREN v. Olden	21, 24, 29
Varney v. Stevens	60
Vinton's Appeal	35, 36

xviii   TABLE OF CASES CITED.

	PAGE		PAGE
Walker's Ex'r v. Walker	17, 18, 35, 36	Wilkinson v. Wilkinson	10
		Willard's Ex'r v. Willard	55, 57
Warden v. Ashburner	78	Williams v. Bradley	59
Waterman v. Alden	23, 31	Williard v. Williard	12
Weeks, Matter of	86	Wilson v. Harman	78
Weld v. Putnam	54	v. Youst	5
Wentz's Appeal	7	Wilson's Appeal	79
Westcott v. Nickerson	55, 57	Wiltbank's Appeal	47
Wethered v. Safe Dep. & Tr. Co.	54	Woodburn's Estate	6
		Wordin's Appeal	62, 63, 67, 68
Wheeler v. Perry	17, 35, 36, 38		
White v. Stanfield	71, 83	Young, Matter of	72, 86
Wiggin v. Swett	73		

THE AMERICAN LAW
RELATING TO
INCOME AND PRINCIPAL.

CHAPTER I.

INTRODUCTION.

INCOME of property consists of the proceeds of what the property produces, the profit which comes from its use in business, or what is paid for its use by another than its owner. Principal, or capital, is the property itself. The absolute owner of the property is likely to treat as income, not only the earnings of the principal property, but all increase which comes from an increase in the value of the property itself, treating as principal what he paid for the property, and as income all excess over the original investment. A person entitled to the use or income of property, or a trustee whose duty it is to pay income to one person or set of persons, holding the principal for others, must be more careful to distinguish between real income and increase which comes from an increase in the value of the property.

The corpus or principal of a trust is not the cash of which it may have originally consisted, or the cash value at the time of appraisal, but the actual property in which it may be invested for the time being. When trust funds are invested in the purchase of shares of stock in a railroad company, the principal is, not the cash paid for the stock, but the stock itself, and if that is later sold for more than the trustee paid for it, the increase is not income but belongs to principal.

The owner of a mine is likely to consider the product of a mine as income. It is not real income, but is part of the property itself. Although timber is a real product of the land, the production of it covers so long a period that a life tenant or a trustee for a life beneficiary cannot ordinarily treat it as income, because the taking of it strips the land of something which cannot be replaced while the life interest lasts. Other kinds of property, usually to a less degree, naturally waste away by being used in the ordinary manner, and the entire product cannot be treated as real income in the strict meaning of the word. There must be deductions from the product from time to time to replace the waste in the principal property.

The owner of property may, of course, give to a person whom he designates as life tenant the right to increase of principal, as well as income, and the full product of timber or mining land, but the word income in a will or deed will be taken in its restricted meaning unless the circumstances or other proper evidence show that he intended to use it in an enlarged sense.

The necessity of distinguishing carefully between income and principal is imposed chiefly upon trustees, and with them it is a matter of great importance; but the same necessity is imposed upon life tenants who have possession and control of the property, and the same general principles apply to both.

CHAPTER II.

WASTING INVESTMENTS.

Income must not consume the Principal. A person entitled to the use and income of property for life, or for a time otherwise limited, must provide for repairing the waste of the corpus which comes from its use or from lapse of time. Similarly, a trustee who holds property under directions to pay the income to one person or set of persons for a time must preserve the principal or corpus of the estate intact from the ordinary processes of waste, by deductions from income. This does not mean that the value of the principal fund must always be kept up out of income; that, in a trust estate or life estate, is usually changing, sometimes increasing and sometimes decreasing. Mere decrease in value should not be made up out of income, nor should increase in value be added to income. Loss of principal by unfortunate investment or by misappropriation of the actual corpus must ordinarily be borne by the principal. But whenever a payment to the trustee or life tenant of what is called income reduces the value of the investment, or whenever the value of the investment decreases from mere lapse of time, part of what is received as income should be added to the principal to repair the waste, unless the intention of the creator of the trust estate or the life estate was opposed. (Balch *v.* Hallet, 10 Gray, 402.)

Leasehold Estates. Rent from a leasehold estate held in trust for the benefit of persons successively interested belongs partly to corpus and only partly to real income, because the value of the leasehold grows less from rent day to rent day and will ultimately be wiped out. (Balch *v.* Hallet, 10 Gray 402; Minot *v.* Thompson, 106 Mass. 583.)

Mines, Quarries, Oil Wells. The products of mines, quarries, or oil wells are really not products, but part of the land itself, which once used cannot be replaced. Such products, therefore, do not come within the strict, narrow meaning of the word income. A life tenant has no right to open new mines, quarries, or wells on the land. If a trustee opens new mines, quarries, or wells, the product, or the rent or royalties, are principal in the absence of any contrary intention on the part of the creator of the trust. He should invest such proceeds and pay the income to those entitled to the use, benefit, or income of the estate. (Blakley *v.* Marshall, 174 Pa. St. 425; Wilson *v.* Youst, 43 W. Va. 826; In re Ridge, 31 Ch. D. 504, 508.)

"Open" Mines. A tenant for life has the right to operate for his own benefit such mines, quarries, or oil wells as were "open" when he came into the estate, and he is entitled to the entire net proceeds. (Koen *v.* Bartlett, 41 W. Va. 559; Spencer *v.* Scurr, 31 Beav. 334.) He may operate such mines, quarries, or wells to exhaustion, without providing for replacing them. (Eley's Appeal, 103 Pa. St. 300; Shoemaker's Appeal, 106 Pa. St. 392.) Similarly a person entitled to the income of land left in trust, on which there were mines, quarries, or wells which were open when the trust estate began or which the trustee was given the right to open by the will creating the trust, is entitled to the net proceeds of the coal or minerals or oil, or to the entire rent or royalties received. No provision need be made to replace the inevitable waste of the corpus. (Woodburn's Estate, 138 Pa. St. 606; Eley's Appeal, 103 Pa. St. 300; McClintock *v.* Dana, 106 Pa. St. 386; Spencer *v.* Scurr, 31 Beav. 334.)

Mines or wells are "open" although the creator of the trust or life estate may not have been operating them himself. For example, if he had leased land for oil purposes, stipulating for the delivery to him of a definite part of the oil produced, a bequest of the income of his estate would include these royalties. (Woodburn's Estate, 138 Pa. St. 606.)

If the will or deed creating the life estate or the trust shows an intention by the testator or grantor that the land is to be used for mining, quarrying, or oil purposes, the use and income will be taken to mean the entire net income without provision to repair waste, unless a contrary intention of the testator or grantor appears. The decisions on this point go wholly on the expressed or implied intention of the grantor or testator. (Eley's Appeal, 103 Pa. St. 300; McClintock *v.* Dana, 106 Pa. St. 386; In re Ridge, 31 Ch. D. 504, 508.)

Where a testator empowered his executors to lease land which he knew to be valuable only as coal land, it was held to be his intention that the entire income from a lease for coal-mining purposes should belong to the life tenant. (Wentz's Appeal, 106 Pa. St. 301. For a similar interpretation of a deed see Bedford's Appeal, 126 Pa. St. 117.)

Timber. The ordinary produce of land, such as crops and fruit, belongs to the persons entitled to income, but timber, although a product of the land, cannot ordinarily be given entirely to a life tenant or to a person entitled to income for a limited or uncertain time. It takes a timber crop so long to mature that it cannot ordinarily be classed as one of the fruits produced during the period of enjoyment of a person whose estate is limited as to time.

It is universal law that a life tenant, legal or equitable, is entitled to cut such timber as is necessary for the repair of buildings and fences on the estate and enough small growth of trees for his own use for firewood. Such timber is known as "estovers" or "botes." (Tiffany on Real Property, Vol. I, p. 566.) A trustee having the possession and control of land partly wooded would need to provide for repairs on the estate out of the woodland, if it were adequate.

This right of estovers is confined to a cutting for use on the estate where the wood was growing, and a life tenant has no right to cut wood for sale, or for use on another estate. (Noyes *v.* Stone, 163 Mass. 490; Armstrong *v.* Wilson, 60 Ill. 226.)

English Law as to Timber. In England by the common law a life tenant, legal or equitable, has certain well-defined rights of profit in woodlands growing on the estate. Except for estovers or botes, a life tenant who is impeachable for waste, and a life tenant is always impeachable for waste unless the settlor or grantor has shown an intention to the contrary, is not entitled to cut timber. Timber under the general law of England includes oak, ash, and elm trees which have reached the age of twenty years, and are not so old as not to contain a reasonable quantity of usable wood in them. In some counties custom has made other kinds of trees timber after they have reached a certain age. If, however, the customary course of management of the property has been to make annual cuttings of timber trees as they became ripe, the life tenant is entitled to make such cuttings and treat them as annual fruits belonging to income. (Honywood *v.* Honywood, L. R. 18 Eq. 306; Dashwood *v.* Magniac, (1891), 3 Ch. 306; In re Harrison's Trusts, L. R. 28 Ch. D. 220.)

A life tenant who is impeachable for waste can cut all wood that is not timber, with certain important exceptions. He cannot cut ornamental trees, or fruit trees, or trees planted to protect banks of streams. He must not cut the stools of underwood. He must not cut those trees which would be timber if they were twenty years old, except for the purpose of thinning in order to allow a proper development of the remaining trees. (Honywood v. Honywood, L. R. 18 Eq. 306.)

These rules laid down in the English courts are obviously suited to a country where the custom prevails of preserving wooded estates as a permanent source of annual income, derived from cutting the timber trees as they ripen, but of seldom entirely clearing the land of woods. The English courts have moreover had opportunity to develop the law from the frequency of life estates and trust estates in landed property.

American Law as to Timber. In this country where the forests are chiefly a natural, rather than a cultivated, growth, and trusts of landed estates are comparatively few, the courts have not yet had much occasion to deal with the problems which have developed the law in England. Our courts nevertheless have always recognized and applied to such cases as have come before them the fundamental principle to be found in the English cases, viz.: that a life tenant or life beneficiary shall not be allowed to use up in his enjoyment of the estate what constitutes the value of the estate, unless it is evident that the grantor or testator intended that he should.

The American courts do not seem to have distinguished between timber and other trees, but seem to have laid down the rule that a life tenant commits waste if he cuts down any trees except what he needs for repairs on the estate or for firewood, and except dead trees and those too old for timber. (Clark *v.* Holden, 7 Gray, 8; Johnson *v.* Johnson, 18 N. H. 594; Smith *v.* Smith, 105 Ga. 106, 111; Modlin *v.* Kennedy, 53 Ind. 267; Stonebraker *v.* Zollickoffer, 52 Md. 154.) But there are many decisions to the effect that if a life tenant cuts down trees in the process of clearing land for cultivation, when it is good husbandry to make such clearing, he is not guilty of waste, and is entitled to the proceeds of the trees if he sells them. The argument is that in a new country the life tenant should not be discouraged from increasing the area of cultivation, and should be allowed to have the proceeds of the trees as a compensation for improving the land. (Smith *v.* Smith, 105 Ga. 106, 111; Sayers *v.* Hoskinson, 110 Pa. St. 473; Wilkinson *v.* Wilkinson, 59 Wis. 557, 561; Keeler *v.* Eastman, 11 Vt. 293; M'Cullough *v.* Irvine's Ex'rs, 13 Pa. St. 438, 443; King *v.* Miller, 99 N. C. 583; Owen *v.* Hyde, 6 Yerg. (Tenn.) 334; Drown *v.* Smith, 52 Maine, 141. Clark *v.* Holden, 7 Gray, 8, seems *contra.*)

It is probable that a life tenant would not be allowed to retain proceeds of timber cut in such a case except when the proceeds over and above the expense of cutting were inconsiderable.

But if the clearing is bad husbandry or if the

trees are cut for the purpose of selling them or of using them off the land, the proceeds belong to the remainderman or to the corpus of the estate. (Johnson v. Johnson, 18 N. H. 594; Smith v. Smith, 105 Ga. 106, 111; Modlin v. Kennedy, 53 Ind. 267; Lester v. Young, 14 R. I. 579; Morehouse v. Cotheal, 22 N. J. Law, 521; Clemence v. Steere, 1 R. I. 272.)

The reasoning, which gives to a life tenant in possession the proceeds of trees cut in the process of clearing the land for its improvement, does not apply to a trustee in possession or control of the land, since he can charge the cost of improvements to the corpus of the estate. On principle a trustee, then, should not give to income the proceeds of timber cut under such circumstances. There are, however, no cases on this point.

Where timber is blown down a tenant for life is absolutely entitled to the proceeds of such as he would have been entitled to cut as thinnings or as ripened timber or for firewood. The proceeds of the other trees are to be invested and the income paid to him. (Bateman v. Hotchkin (No. 2), 31 Beav. 486; In re Harrison's Trusts, L. R. 28 Ch. D. 220; Stonebraker v. Zollickoffer, 52 Md. 154.)[1]

---

[1] In Stonebraker v. Zollickoffer, 52 Md. 154, a storm of wind had blown down a large quantity of timber. The trustee converted part of this into cooper-stuff and sold it, selling the remainder for firewood. It was held that the proceeds of the cooper-stuff belonged to principal, and that the proceeds of the firewood belonged to income for the life tenant upon the supposition that nothing

A life tenant, in the absence of anything in the will or deed to show a contrary intention of the testator or grantor, has the right to cut wood as a source of profit in the manner customary on the estate before his interest was established. (Williard *v.* Williard, 56 Pa. St. 119; Findlay *v.* Smith, 6 Munf. (Va). 134; Dashwood *v.* Magniac, L. R. (1891) 3 Ch. 306.) Thus in Findlay *v.* Smith where a testator devised to his wife for life an estate on which there were salt works, giving her power to operate the salt works for her benefit, it was held that the widow had the right to cut from the estate all the wood that she needed for fuel in the operation of the salt works and was not limited to the quantity used by the testator. It had been his custom to cut from the estate all the fuel he needed for that purpose.

Such customary use may authorize the life tenant even to clear the land of the timber, and a bequest of the income of timber land which the testator himself was in the process of clearing would probably be taken to include the entire net proceeds of the timber. (Williard *v.* Williard, 56 Pa. St. 119.) Such timber land would probably be treated just as open mines are treated, although the income from which was valuable as timber had been converted into firewood. The tenant for life is entitled to old trees which cannot be used as timber, and to the tops and smaller branches of trees which are felled for timber, and to the regular thinnings and trimmings of trees in the woods. He may sell them, and, if he does, is entitled to the proceeds.

it is exhausting the corpus. It is a question of the testator's or grantor's intention. (Eley's Appeal, 103 Pa. St. 300 ; Bedford's Appeal, 126 Pa. St. 117.)

Bonds bought at a Premium. To a certain extent bonds bought at a premium are a wasting investment, because if they are held until maturity the premium will be entirely lost, and, even if they are not held until maturity, other things being equal, the premium will gradually grow smaller as maturity approaches. Accordingly it has been held in some jurisdictions that a trustee who has purchased bonds at a premium should deduct from the various collections of interest and add to the principal such sums as will replace the premium if the bonds are held until maturity. That is, he should establish a sort of sinking fund to repair the waste of principal. (New England Trust Co. *v.* Eaton, 140 Mass. 532 ; N. Y. Life Insurance & Trust Co. *v.* Baker, 165 N. Y. 484 ; In re Allis' Estate, 101 N. W. 365 (Wis. Nov. 15, 1904.) *Contra,* Matter of Johnson, 57 App. Div. (N. Y.) 494, 502.) This should be done although the bonds will not mature until after the termination of the trust. (In re Allis' Estate, 101 N. W. 365.)

If after this is done the bonds should be sold at a larger premium than was paid for them, it has been held that the premium received belongs to the principal, and also such of the sinking fund as has already been accumulated. The entire increase in value, representing the excess over the cost and the sinking fund already accumulated, is regarded as an increase in the value of the corpus. (New England Trust Co. v. Eaton, 140 Mass. 532.)[1]

[1] NOTE ON THE MASSACHUSETTS LAW. There is some doubt whether the case of New England Trust Co. v. Eaton, 140 Mass. 532, goes to the extent of establishing the rule that a trustee *must* provide a sinking fund to replace premiums. The actual decision goes no further than that a trustee who has done so has acted properly. In a previously decided case, Hemenway v. Hemenway, 134 Mass. 446, which was a bill for instructions by trustees under a will, the trustees had bought a comparatively few railroad bonds at a small premium. The court refused to lay down any general rule which would control all cases of bonds bought at a premium, but said, " The trustee, who has the fund always in his hands and under his eyes, must take reasonable care to hold the balance even between opposing interests." It was found as a fact in this case that the balance had been evenly held between the persons entitled to the income and those entitled to the corpus. So the court held that the fact that a small premium was paid was not of itself alone enough to prevent those entitled to income from receiving the entire net income.

Hemenway v. Hemenway was not expressly overruled by New England Trust Co. v. Eaton, although the court had the case clearly in mind. There was a strong dissenting opinion, concurred in by three judges out of a total of seven, upon the reasoning of Hemenway v. Hemenway. The language of New England Trust Co. v. Eaton was however very strong: " There can ordinarily be no better test of the true income which a sum of money will produce, having regard to the rights of both the tenant for life and the remainderman, than the interest which can be received from a bond which sells above par and is payable at the termination of a fixed time, deducting from such interest, as it becomes due, such sums as will at maturity efface the premium. If such a bond has increased in value since its purchase, assuming it to have been an entirely safe investment, and none other should be made, it is because a change in the rates of interest, or some similar cause, has altered market values;" per Devens, J.

Under the circumstances the safe course for trustees to follow in

Other jurisdictions have held that no part of the current income should be used to replace a premium. (Hite's Devisees *v.* Hite's Ex'r, 93 Ky. 257; Penn-Gaskell's Estate (No. 2), 208 Pa. St. 346.) It is argued that gains and losses in the value of bonds should come within the general rule applied to other securities: that they are gains and losses in corpus. It is pointed out that premiums are not paid to secure greater income, but usually represent safety and permanency of the investment and facility of transfer and use, and in fact usually accompany a low rate of interest. It is argued that the premium is paid more for the interest of the remainderman than for the interest of the life tenant, and so should be considered as something that the fund itself should endure, as being a charge for the benefit of the whole fund. (Penn-Gaskell's Estate (No. 2), 208 Pa. St. 346; N. E. Trust Co. *v.* Eaton, 140 Mass. 532, 545 (dissenting opinion by Holmes, J.).)

If the intention of the creator of the life estate or of the trust estate appears to have been that wasting premiums should not be replaced out of income, of course that intention controls. If the main object

---

Massachusetts would seem to be, to set aside a porportional part of each interest payment to replace the premium paid by them.

The following quotation from Loring's "A Trustee's Handbook" (2d ed.), p. 112, indicates the practice and opinion of a Massachusetts trustee of large practical experience: "The practice of buying bonds which sell at a discount, to balance those bought at a premium, is not sound, as the difference of price is not simply a question of interest, but is more often one of security, nor can the loss on one investment be set off against the gain on another."

of a testator appears to have been to provide a liberal income consistent with safety, the courts will incline to the view that he did not intend any deductions from income to replace such loss of corpus. (Matter of Hoyt, 160 N. Y. 607.) A direction by a testator to invest in certain kinds of bonds and pay to his four sons "all the dividends and income" of said bonds, over and above the expense of carrying out the trust, was held to indicate an intention that no deductions from income of such bonds should be made to replace the premiums which the trustee was obliged to pay. (Shaw v. Cordis, 143 Mass. 443.)

Where bonds which are rated at a premium are part of the identical property left by the testator, and the trustees have properly allowed the investment to remain, deductions should not be made from current income to replace the wasting premium, unless it appears that the testator intended that such provision should be made. (Sargent v. Sargent, 103 Mass. 297. See also Reed v. Head, 6 Allen, 174.)

Profit on a Sale of Bonds. If bonds are sold at a larger premium than was paid for them, all of the increase belongs to the principal, and none of the gain can be said to be income. (Matter of Proctor, 85 Hun, 572; Matter of Gerry, 103 N. Y. 445; Graham's Estate, 198 Pa. St. 216. But see Park's Estate, 173 Pa. St. 190.)

CHAPTER III.

DIVIDENDS ON SHARES OF STOCK.

IN determining whether dividends on shares of stock in corporations or joint-stock companies are income or are wholly or partly corpus, the same general principle of preserving the corpus intact and not using it up as income applies as in other investments. If dividends are not paid out of earnings, but are really divisions of the capital of the corporation or company they constitute part of the principal of the trust, and should not be treated as income in the absence of a contrary intention of the creator of the trust. (Heard *v.* Eldredge, 109 Mass. 258; Wheeler *v.* Perry, 18 N. H. 307; Walker's Ex'r *v.* Walker, 68 N. H. 407.)

Income of Corporation and Income of Stockholder. The profits and earnings of a corporation or joint stock company are income of the corporation or company as soon as they are made, but they are not income of the stockholder until the corporation has set them apart as dividend. (Minot *v.* Paine, 99 Mass. 101.) As a matter of good business policy it is left very much to the discretion of the officers of corporations to determine what portion of earnings to divide among the stockholders, what portion to expend for enlargements of the working capital, and what portion to accumulate for any reason. It has not been the policy of the courts to interfere with a very free exercise of this discretion so long as good faith is apparent. In the exercise of this discretion, directors of a corporation would not be required to consider the relative rights of persons entitled to income and those entitled to corpus. (Gibbons v. Mahon, 136 U. S. 549; Rand v. Hubbell, 115 Mass. 461; Davis v. Jackson, 152 Mass. 58.)

Inasmuch as the officers of a corporation ordinarily have no right to use up the fundamental capital of the corporation in dividends, a dividend is presumed to be from earnings unless the contrary is clearly shown. (Walker's Ex'r v. Walker, 68 N. H. 407; Smith v. Dana, 60 At. Rep. 117 (Conn. Mar. 9, 1905).)

Regular Dividends. This is especially true of the regular dividends. For the purposes of determining what is principal and what income, it will be assumed that the directors are making proper provision out of their gross income for the waste of the plant or other form of capital. Trustees can therefore safely treat regular dividends as belonging to income at the time when they are declared, even though they may know that the company lost money during the period for which the dividends were declared. It is part of the business policy of the officers of corporations to have their regular dividends uniform in amount. So they retain enough of the profits of good years to make up the deficiency of poor years. (Cook on Corporations, 5th ed. § 547.)

As it is the declaration of the dividend which gives the stockholder a right to it, it is general law that the owner of the stock, or the person entitled to the income of the stock at the time the regular dividend is declared, is entitled to the whole dividend; no inquiry is made as to when the earnings were made and usually no attempt is made to apportion regular dividends as to time. (See authorities *infra*, under Apportionment of Current Income.)

Wasting Dividends. Where, however, it is clear that the regular dividends are wearing away the capital of the corporation, a trustee would need to provide for a repair of this gradual waste of his principal, unless a different intention is found in the instrument creating the trust. An investment by the trustee himself in stock of a corporation which had a right so to waste its capital would ordinarily not be a proper investment. If the trust property comes to him already invested in such stock, and he has authority to continue the investment, the chances are strong that the creator of the trust intended the entire dividends to be treated as income. Thus in the case of Reed *v.* Head, 6 Allen, 174, a testator had left the income of certain shares of stock in a land company to certain persons for life. The dividends regularly paid to the testator and to the life tenants were partly out of the corpus. It was held that the life tenants were entitled to the whole dividends, although these dividends were wasting the principal, because this was evidently the testator's intention, for the custom of the company during his lifetime had been to pay out in dividends the proceeds of property which constituted capital of the company.

Extraordinary Cash Dividends. Extraordinary dividends present much more perplexing questions to a trustee, and there is a hopeless conflict of authority on several important points involved. Although the general rule of preserving the corpus intact and of giving earnings to income applies in the case of extraordinary dividends, a serious difficulty arises from the fact that extraordinary dividends are not usually based upon current earnings. Very often a large part of the earnings on which such a dividend is based have been accumulated before the shares of stock came into the hands of the trustee, and were represented in the value of the shares at the time the trustee acquired them.

For although undivided earnings of a corporation are not the property of the stockholder and so are not income as to him while they remain undivided, he of course has an interest in them, as he has in all the property of the corporation. The existence of undivided earnings increases the value of each share of stock, and for this reason they are in one sense capital of the stockholder. (Gibbons *v.* Mahon, 136 U. S. 549; Rand *v.* Hubbell, 115 Mass. 461; Matter of Kernochan, 104 N. Y. 618; Second Universalist Church *v.* Colegrove, 74 Conn. 79; Gifford *v.* Thompson, 115 Mass. 478; Van Doren *v.* Olden, 19 N. J. Eq. 176.)

Apportionment of Extraordinary Cash Dividends. This double nature of undivided earnings which are really income, but which by being retained have increased the value of the shares of stock, has caused the courts a great deal of difficulty, because a dividend out of accumulated earnings will proportionately reduce the value of each share of stock. Where the accumulation of income has been going on for many years, as is often the case, and a large extraordinary cash dividend is declared, the effect of which must be greatly to impair the value of shares of stock, should such a dividend be treated by a trustee as income to be paid to the life beneficiary ? It is a dividend from income of the corporation, but at the same time it reduces the value of the corpus. To illustrate, assume that a father has left to trustees, to pay the income thereof to his son for life, shares of stock in a mining company which has for years been accumulating undivided earnings. Partly as a result of this accumulation the value of the shares is about $200. A year after the father's death the corporation divides these surplus earnings in the form of a cash dividend of $75 a share. The value of the shares is thereby reduced to $125. Should this $75 a share be paid over to the son as income, or should it be held by the trustee as part of the corpus? Complicate the situation somewhat by assuming that the dividend is declared ten years after the father's death, and that part of the earnings has been accumulating during that time. Assume still again that all of the accumulation has taken place after the father's death, and that the dividend had been declared the day after the son's death. Should any part of the extra dividend be paid to the estate of the son during whose life it was earned?

Massachusetts Rule, against Apportionment of Extra Dividends. It is not surprising that widely different rules have been developed by different jurisdictions. Some jurisdictions have adhered to the common-law rule that dividends cannot be apportioned as to time. Their reasoning is that earnings of a corporation do not become income of the stockholder until they are declared as dividends, and that there should be no inquiry as to when the corporation made the earnings. They argue that it is impracticable for a trustee or for the court to go deeply enough into the affairs of a corporation in such a collateral matter, to determine justly when the basis of the dividend accrued to the corporation. They hold that the only inquiry should be whether the basis of the dividend is earnings which have not been actually capitalized, or capital of the corporation, and that if the dividend is actually from earnings, it is the declaration by the officers of the corporation which makes it income. (Rand *v.* Hubbell, 115 Mass. 461; Minot *v.* Paine, 99 Mass. 101; Gifford *v.* Thompson, 115 Mass. 478; Hemenway *v.* Hemenway, 181 Mass. 406; Adams *v.* Adams, 139 Mass. 449, 452; Richardson *v.* Richardson, 75 Maine, 570; Waterman *v.* Alden, 42 Ill. App. 294; 144 Ill. 90; De Koven *v.* Alsop, 205 Ill. 309; Hite's Devisees *v.* Hite's Ex'r, 93 Ky. 257; Second Universalist Church *v.* Colegrove, 74 Conn. 79; Matter of Kernochan, 104 N. Y. 618; Gibbons *v.* Mahon, 136 U. S. 549; see Gen. Statutes Conn. (Rev. of 1902), § 377; see also Millen *v.* Guerrard, 67 Ga. 284.)

It has also been held as a corollary of this doctrine that if a corporation comes to final liquidation with a surplus of undivided earnings which have not been capitalized and makes a distribution of the property of the corporation in a large final dividend without a separation of earnings from capital, the whole dividend should be treated as belonging to principal, because there has been no declaration of a dividend from earnings as earnings. (Gifford *v.* Thompson, 115 Mass. 478; Second Universalist Church *v.* Colegrove, 74 Conn. 79; In re Armitage, L. R. (1893) 3 Ch. 337.)

Pennsylvania Rule of Apportionment of Extra Dividends. On the other hand, there are jurisdictions which hold just as firmly that the trustee or life-tenant and the courts should, in justice to the conflicting interests and to the intention of testators or other creators of the limited estates, apportion these extraordinary dividends according to the time when the earnings were actually made. It is argued that earnings accumulated during the life of a testator, or before the stock was bought by a trustee, are represented in the value of the securities, and to give such a dividend to income would seriously impair the corpus of the estate and do grave violence to the intention of the testator and to the interests of the remainderman, and in many cases to the real interests of the life beneficiaries. It is urged with great force that when testators speak of "profits and income" they mean only such as are made by the corporation after the trust is established. (Earp's Appeal, 28 Pa. St. 368; Smith's Estate, 140 Pa. St. 344; Van Doren *v.* Olden, 19 N. J. Eq. 176; Lang's Ex'r *v.* Lang, 56 N. J. Eq. 603; Thomas *v.* Gregg, 78 Md. 545; Cobb *v.* Fant, 36 S. C. 1. See Gen. Statutes of Conn. (Rev. of 1902), § 377. See also Pritchitt *v.* Nashville Trust Co., 96 Tenn. 472.)[1]

One of the chief criticisms of the Pennsylvania rule, as it is called, is the inability to carry it to its logical conclusion. If the earnings as they accumulate belong equitably to the person entitled to income, why should he not receive part of the price obtained for stock held during a period of accumulation and sold before any dividend is declared? No court has yet applied the rule to such a case. (Connolly's Estate (No. 1), 198 Pa. St. 137.) Nor

[1] In England the Apportionment Act of 1870 requires all dividends of public companies to be apportioned as if they accrued from day to day. (33 & 34 Vict. c. 35.)

DIVIDENDS ON SHARES OF STOCK. 25

is a person who is entitled to income during a limited time ever given any part of either cash or stock dividend declared after his estate has ceased, although the dividend may be based upon earnings accumulated during the time he was entitled to income. (Bates *v.* Mackinley, 31 Beav. 280.)

It must however be confessed that the Pennsylvania rule, so far as it can be applied, comes nearer just results than the more strictly logical and more convenient rule of the Massachusetts courts. (See Davis *v.* Jackson, 152 Mass. 58.)[1]

Stock Dividends. Closely akin to this question, and involving to some extent the same arguments, is the question of stock dividends. Stock dividends are dividends in the form of new stock in the corporation issued to the stockholders because of an increase of the working capital. The usual reason for the issue of stock dividends is because the corporation has increased its working capital by the addition of undivided earnings. Usually the directors of a corporation have the right to decide what part of the earnings, if any, they shall distribute,

---

[1] In Quinn *v.* Safe Deposit & Trust Co., 93 Md. 285, a sinking fund had been accumulated for the payment of certain bonds which the company had secured. The accumulation took place almost wholly before the establishment of the trust. The fund being unexpectedly set free by the payment of the bonds by another company, a cash dividend was declared out of part of this fund. It was held that the entire dividend belonged to current income. The accumulation was under such circumstances that it could not increase the value of the shares of stock, so that the reason for giving it to principal did not exist.

what part they shall simply accumulate as a surplus and what part they shall use in increasing the plant or in betterments. If the actual capital is increased out of earnings, it is not usually necessary that new stock should be issued to indicate the increase. Any increase in the property of the corporation in whatever form would usually increase proportionately the value of the shares of stock.

Massachusetts Rule as to Stock Dividends. It is obvious that a stock dividend is not a distribution by the corporation of any of its tangible property and is not a gain by the stockholder in any tangible property, for although he has more shares of stock he has no greater proportion of the total number of shares. For this reason many courts have held that stock dividends are not income. If they are issued because of any increase of value it is because of an increase in the capital of the corporation. It is argued that it is immaterial that the increase in the capital came out of earnings, because the undivided earnings of the corporation are not income of a stockholder. It is further pointed out that if the undivided earnings were simply accumulated, whether capitalized or not, without any stock dividend, no court would hold that any part of the increased value of each share of stock belonged to income, even though the stock were sold at its increased value a month before the stock dividend was declared. (Minot *v.* Paine, 99 Mass. 101; D'Ooge *v.* Leeds, 176 Mass. 558; Daland *v.* Williams, 101

Mass. 571; Adams v. Adams, 139 Mass. 449, 452; Rand v. Hubbell, 115 Mass. 461; Gibbons v. Mahon, 136 U. S. 549; De Koven v. Alsop, 205 Ill. 309; Spooner v. Phillips, 62 Conn. 62; Second Universalist Church v. Colegrove, 74 Conn. 79; Richardson v. Richardson, 75 Maine, 570; Brown & Larned, Petitioners, 14 R. I. 371; Greene v. Smith, 17 R. I. 28; Bouch v. Sproule, L. R. 12 App. Cas. 385.)[1]

[1] "Reserved and accumulated earnings, so long as they are held and invested by the corporation, being part of its corporate property, it follows that the interest therein, represented by each share, is capital, and not income, of that share, as between the tenant for life and the remainderman, legal or equitable, thereof.

Whether the gains and profits of a corporation should be so invested and apportioned as to increase the value of each share of stock, for the benefit of all persons interested in it, either for a term of life or for years, or by way of remainder in fee; or should be distributed and paid out as income, to the tenant for life or for years, excluding the remainderman from any participation therein; is a question to be determined by the action of the corporation itself, at such times and in such manner as the fair and honest administration of its whole property and business may require or permit, and by a rule applicable to all holders of like shares of its stock; and cannot, without producing great embarrassment and inconvenience, be left open to be tried and determined by the courts, as often as it may be litigated between persons claiming successive interests under a trust created by the will of a single shareholder, and by a distinct and separate investigation, through a master in chancery or otherwise, of the affairs and accounts of the corporation, as of the dates when the provisions of the will of that shareholder take effect, and with regard to his shares only. . . .

A stock dividend really takes nothing from the property of the corporation, and adds nothing to the interests of the shareholders. Its property is not diminished, and their interests are not increased. After such a dividend, as before, the corporation has the title in all the corporate property; the aggregate interests therein of all the

Pennsylvania Rule as to Stock Dividends. On the other hand there are several jurisdictions which are bound to the doctrine that a stock dividend belongs to income in so far as it is based upon earnings accumulated while the original stock was part of the trust estate. All of the jurisdictions which apportion extraordinary cash dividends would probably apportion stock dividends on a like basis, if they are based to any extent upon earnings made while the trust estate owned the stock.

The argument is that, as the earnings accumulate, the stockholder has an equitable right to them as income, and the form of the dividend which may later be declared should not deprive him of this right. The declaration of a cash dividend gives him the actual earnings; the declaration of a stock dividend signifies that these earnings have been irrevocably devoted to capital, and the new stock represents them. The new stock can be sold for approximately what the cash dividend would have amounted to, and the transaction of making a stock dividend is not essentially different from a declaration of a cash dividend and a sale of enough new stock to exactly use up the dividend. It is further argued that no rule of convenience should allow the officers of cor-

shareholders are represented by the whole number of shares; and the proportional interest of each shareholder remains the same. The only change is in the evidence which represents that interest, the new shares and the original shares together representing the same proportional interest that the original shares represented before the issue of new ones." Gray, J., in Gibbons *v.* Mahon, 136 U. S. 549, 558.

porations to determine the rights of those entitled to income and those entitled to corpus. (Earp's Appeal, 28 Pa. St. 368; Smith's Estate, 140 Pa. St. 344; Ashhurst *v.* Field's Adm'r, 26 N. J. Eq. 1, 11; Van Doren *v.* Olden, 19 N. J. Eq. 176; Lang's Ex'r *v.* Lang, 56 N. J. Eq. 603; Thomas *v.* Gregg, 78 Md. 545; Pritchitt *v.* Nashville Trust Co., 96 Tenn. 472. See also Cobb *v.* Fant, 36. S C. 1; Lord *v.* Brooks, 52 N. H. 72; Peirce *v.* Burroughs, 58 N. H. 302.)

Method of Apportionment. The method of apportionment adopted in Earp's Appeal, the leading case for this doctrine, was to find the difference in value between the old stock owned by the trust at the date when the trust was established and the old and the new stock together at the time of the stock dividend. The surplus earnings being left as large as when the trust began, the increase in value was held to belong to income. Thus it was found that the original 540 shares were worth $67,500 at the time of the testator's death. These original shares together with the 810 new shares of the dividend were worth $108,000 at the time of the stock dividend. The difference, $40,500, representing 506 new shares at market value, was held to be profit which arose since the death of the testator, and was apportioned entirely to income, since the stock dividend did not reduce the surplus earnings below what they were at the beginning of the trust.

This seems to be the accepted method of apportioning a stock dividend. It will be noticed that only a part of the new shares was given to income, although it was found that the stock dividend was based wholly upon earnings made while the trust owned the stock. The life tenant ought never to get more than the par value of all the new stock issued to his trustee, although the new stock is worth more than par. The reason that it is worth more than par is usually because of a large fund of undivided earnings which are not being permanently capitalized and in which it has equal equities with the old stock. The stock dividend represents a permanent capitalization only of earnings equal to the par value of the new stock. To illustrate with the facts of Earp's Appeal, if the life tenant had been given the entire issue of 810 shares which sold at $80, he would have had a dividend of $64,800 in value. The original 540 shares left as principal would have been worth only $43,200, a shrinkage of $24,200. Instead, he was given enough of the new stock at its market value to equal the 810 new shares at $50, the par value.

In making the apportionment the periodical fiscal reports, usually semi-annual or annual, of the corporation are usually taken, as showing when the earnings were accumulated, and no attempt is made to apportion for periods less than those covered by such reports. (Earp's Appeal, 28 Pa. St. 368; Thomas *v.* Gregg, 78 Md. 545.)

New York Rule as to Stock Dividends. Some

jurisdictions which have refused to apportion extraordinary dividends give the entire stock dividend to income if it is based upon earnings, regardless of when the earnings were accumulated. (McLouth v. Hunt, 154 N. Y. 179; Lowry v. Farmers' Loan & Trust Co., 172 N. Y. 137; Hite's Devisees v. Hite's Ex'r, 93 Ky. 257; see also Millen v. Guerrard, 67 Ga. 284.)[1]

Option to take Cash or New Stock. When stockholders are given an option to take their dividend out of earnings from the company either in cash or in new stock of the same value, courts which adhere to the Massachusetts rule have held that the dividend should be treated as a cash dividend and should go to income, even though it is actually taken in the form of new stock. Such a transaction is treated as in substance the declaration of a cash dividend and a simultaneous sale by the company of new stock. (Davis v. Jackson, 152 Mass. 58; Lyman v. Pratt, 183 Mass. 58; Waterman v. Alden, 42 Ill. App. 294, 144 Ill. 90; see also In re Malam, L. R. (1894) 3 Ch. 578.)[2]

[1] The language of the New York cases indicates that the courts would probably not give to the life tenant a stock dividend out of earnings accumulated mostly during the life of a testator, unless they found evidences of intention that the life tenant should have such a dividend. The New York courts have reserved to themselves considerable discretion in applying any rule. (McLouth v. Hunt, 154 N. Y. 179; Lowry v. Farmers' Loan & Trust Co., 172 N. Y. 137.)

[2] In Davis v. Jackson, 152 Mass. 58, the stockholders of a corporation voted to increase the capital stock by 1,000 shares of $100

If, however, this is simply a form adopted by the corporation of issuing a stock dividend and the option is only apparent, or if the choice of cash involves giving up without adequate compensation the right to subscribe for new stock at less than the market value, so that no prudent man would avail himself of it, Massachusetts courts have held that

<blockquote>
each, and that each stockholder be entitled to subscribe for one new share for every four held by him. At a meeting of the directors held on the same day at the close of the stockholders' meeting an extra dividend of $25 a share out of the earnings was declared. This dividend was by design exactly sufficient to enable the stockholders to pay for their new stock if they wished, but they were not bound to take new stock, and could take the cash and sell their rights to subscribe for new stock. The earnings of the company were sufficient to pay the dividend, but if they were so used, then it would be necessary to raise about an equal amount to pay for additions which had already been made to the working capital and which had increased its value at least twenty-five per cent above the par value of the old stock. The directors had discussed the question of a stock dividend and, with the understanding that a stock dividend was not permitted by law, had used this method as a substitute.

Held that the dividend was income to the stockholders. "The dividend was declared as a cash dividend, and it represented what originally at least were earnings of the company. In justice the earnings of the company ought to go to the life tenants. If the only thing to be considered by the corporation was the relation between tenants for life and remainder men, it would have no right to devote income to increasing capital; if it wished to increase its plant, it would have to do it by borrowing money or by issuing more stock. In fact it has the right to appropriate income to permanent improvements, because it has the right to manage its affairs in the way it deems best for them, but when the form of the transaction has not that effect there is no reason why courts should be astute to bring it out." Holmes, J., pp. 59, 60.
</blockquote>

the dividend is a stock dividend and should belong to principal. (Daland *v.* Williams, 101 Mass. 571; Rand *v.* Hubbell, 115 Mass. 461; see also Bouch *v.* Sproule, L. R. 12 App. Cas. 385.)

A division by the corporation of its own old stock, in which it has invested surplus earnings, has been held to be equivalent to a cash dividend and to belong wholly to income. (Leland *v.* Hayden, 102 Mass. 542.) But if the corporation has paid for such old stock with money raised by an issue of bonds, so that the distribution of the stock actually impairs its fundamental capital, the old stock should be credited to principal. (Gilkey *v.* Paine, 80 Maine, 319.)

A dividend in the form of interest-bearing bonds, based upon a fund of accumulated earnings which are retained by the company, has been held to belong to the principal of a trust fund, because no property was taken out of the business or was changed in its relation to the business. (D'Ooge *v.* Leeds, 176 Mass. 558; see also Mills, Adm'r *v.* Britton, 64 Conn. 4.) Followers of the Pennsylvania rule and of the New York rule would have given such a dividend partly or wholly to income.

Delayed Dividends. A distinction must be made between extraordinary dividends and large dividends which are simply delayed payments of guaranteed regular dividends. In Meldrin *v.* Trustees of Trinity Church, 100 Ga. 479, lessees of a railroad agreed with the lessor corporation to declare, and pay to the latter's stockholders, semi-annual dividends of seven per cent, but for several years they failed to do it. A successor, under the lease, of the lessee corporation later paid over a portion of these back dividends. A life tenant of stock had meanwhile died. It was held that his estate was entitled to these back dividends which should have been paid during his life. The dividends were not undeclared, but were predeclared up to seven per cent by the contract between the corporations.

Dividends out of Capital. The same general principles against impairment of the capital of the corporation apply to extraordinary dividends as to regular dividends. Moreover the courts are much less likely in case of an extraordinary dividend to assume that it is paid out of earnings or profits, although the officers of a corporation will be allowed within reasonable limits to decide what are earnings or profits and what capital. The vote declaring an extraordinary dividend usually specifies in more or less definite terms the source from which the dividend is paid, and if there is such a vote the statement therein of the source of the dividend would seldom, if ever, be questioned in a proceeding to determine whether or not the dividend belongs to principal or to income.

Meaning of the Word Capital. Some confusion has been caused by the indefiniteness of the word *capital*. Some courts have used it to mean what may be called for the sake of clearness the "fundamental capital," including only so much of the property of the corporation as may be said to represent the capital stock, being the original investment of the stockholders with such additions from earnings as were necessary to repair waste and such other additions to working capital as have formed the basis for new issues of shares. Some opinions have used the term to include all the property of the corporation, whether used in the business or not. Others include in capital proper only such property of the corporation as is actually used in the business of the corporation: that is, the "working capital." Other property, made up of surplus profits invested to produce income outside the corporation's business has sometimes been called "floating capital." (Clark & Marshall, Private Corporations, Vol. II, § 375.)

Dividends which reduce Fundamental Capital. Dividends out of the proceeds of fundamental capital, whether on final liquidation of the corporation's affairs, or on a partial liquidation, are a repayment of the original investment which is represented by the capital stock, and so belong to the corpus or principal of a trust fund. (Walker's Ex'r v. Walker, 68 N. H. 407; Vinton's Appeal, 99 Pa. St. 434; Wheeler v. Perry, 18 N. H. 307; Mercer v. Buchanan, 132 Fed. Rep. 501; Heard v. Eldredge, 109 Mass. 258.)

Where a wharf company, whose regular income consisted of rents and wharfage, divided among stockholders part of a sum received from the city for real estate taken by right of eminent domain, the dividend was held to have been paid out of capital and for that reason to belong entirely to principal. (Heard *v.* Eldredge, 109 Mass. 258.)

It makes no difference that the property sold is no longer needed in the regular business. If it represented fundamental capital the proceeds of it are capital, and, although it may be proper for the corporation to pay the proceeds out as dividend, the dividend is not income. (Wheeler *v.* Perry, 18 N. H. 307; Walker's Ex'r *v.* Walker, 68 N. H. 407; Vinton's Appeal, 99 Pa. St. 434.) It is also immaterial that the value of the capital which the corporation retains is as large as, or even many times larger than, the sum total of its capital stock at par. (Mercer *v.* Buchanan, 132 Fed. Rep. 501; Matter of Rogers, 161 N. Y. 108; Wheeler *v.* Perry, 18 N. H. 307.)

Several cases have come before the courts in recent years growing out of the frequent mergers of corporations. It may be of profit to examine briefly the essential facts of one or two of these cases. In Mercer *v.* Buchanan, 132 Fed. Rep. 501, a corporation, the A. Co., with a capital of $2,000,000 was engaged chiefly in the manufacture of sheet steel. It also owned the stock of several subsidiary companies which paid dividends. The A. Co. sold its sheet steel plant and one of the subsidiary companies to the American Sheet Steel Co. for $6,000,000 in preferred stock of the latter company, $6,000,000 in common stock and $1,119,000 in cash for mate-

DIVIDENDS ON SHARES OF STOCK. 37

rial on hand and in course of manufacture. The A. Co. agreed not to engage in the manufacture of sheet steel for fifteen years. It retained several subsidiary companies and announced to its stockholders its intention of continuing the business of these companies, and expressed an expectation of earning good profits. Out of the proceeds of this sale a cash dividend of fifty per cent was declared, amounting to $1,000,000. $3,000,000 of the preferred stock of the American Company, and $6,000,000 of the common stock was also divided up as dividend. It was held that these dividends were all paid out of the proceeds of the capital of the A. Co. and for that reason belonged entirely to the principal of the trust fund.

In Smith v. Hooper, 95 Md. 16, a testator had bequeathed $10,000 to a trustee to pay the "dividends and income" to M. for life. At M.'s request the trustees used the $10,000 to purchase the property of a can manufactory. This property was then transferred to a corporation, the trustees taking 300 shares of stock in payment. They sold half of these shares for $5,000, and invested part of this $5,000 in stock of another can company. The companies paid large dividends, which the trustees paid to M. as income. Both corporations were later absorbed by the A. Co., and, as a result, the trustees received a large block of shares in the A. Co. The original trust fund of $10,000 has increased to a value of $158,000, part of which is proceeds of stock sold and part of stock received on transfer of the original stock. It was held that none of this increase could be called income, and that it belonged wholly to the corpus of the estate. Although there had been a large profit, the profit came from the increase in value of the stock. "Increase and income are not synonymous terms. Until detached or separated from the shares whose value it enhances, increase forms part of that value, and, therefore, part of the shares; and if it be part of the shares themselves, then, whilst it may be *profit*, it is in no sense income."

Dividends by Land Companies. Profits accruing to the corporation by reason of the increase in value of the property in which its fundamental capital was invested are not income, but are accretions to capital, except in cases where it is part of the regular business of the corporation to make profits out of such investments. Thus a profit due to the increase in value of land bought by a manufacturing corporation with its fundamental capital for the site of part of its plant is an accretion to capital and does not belong to the income of shareholders when paid to them in dividends. (Wheeler *v.* Perry, 18 N. H. 307; Smith *v.* Hooper, 95 Md. 16; Mercer *v.* Buchanan, 132 Fed. Rep. 501.)

But when trustees hold stock in a land company part of whose regular business is to buy and sell land for a profit, a dividend based upon profits due to an increase in value of land while owned by the company and realized on a sale of the land is properly income. Land in such a case is being dealt in as a commodity, and the capital which should be kept intact is only what is represented by the purchase price plus the expense of holding the land. (Thompson's Estate, 153 Pa. St. 332; Oliver's Estate, 136 Pa. St. 43.) The income is held to accrue at the time the profit is realized, that is at the time of the sale. (Oliver's Estate, 136 Pa. St. 43.)

Where a corporation, engaged as a regular business in purchasing land, filling up flats, laying out streets, erecting, leasing, and selling warehouses, has declared a dividend based partly upon proceeds of land sold by the corporation, the dividend has been held to belong to income, to which a life beneficiary was entitled in the absence of any facts showing that the dividend was part of the capital of the corporation or that the payment impaired or diminished the value of the shares. (Balch v. Hallet, 10 Gray 402.)

Capitalized Earnings. Accumulated earnings which are made the basis of an addition to the capital stock become thereby part of the fundamental capital and cannot thereafter be divided as income. After the new issue of stock the property, although derived from earnings, represents permanent capital of the stockholder. (Hemenway v. Hemenway, 181 Mass. 406; Smith v. Dana, 60 At. Rep. 117 (Conn. Mar. 9, 1905).)

Dividends from Floating Capital. Earnings do not

become part of the permanent capital of the corporation by simply being accumulated and even temporarily invested outside the business of the company. So long as their identity is preserved they constitute a fund from which the directors can at discretion declare a dividend which is a dividend from income of the corporation. States which do not apportion extraordinary dividends would give such a dividend entirely to income. (Matter of Rogers, 161 N. Y. 108; Hemenway v. Hemenway, 181 Mass. 406; see also Quinn v. Safe Deposit & Trust Co., 93 Md. 285.)

Where a company engaged in the business of mining and selling coal had accumulated a large fund of undivided earnings, part of which stood on its books as a "Coal Land Renewal Fund," and had been held in reserve for the purpose of purchasing new mines as the old ones became exhausted, and part of which was simply surplus profits, most of which fund was invested to produce income in stocks, bonds, and other securities, a large cash dividend based upon these accumulated earnings was held to be a dividend belonging to income. (Hemenway v. Hemenway, 181 Mass. 406.)[1]

[1] For a different interpretation of the same facts see Second Universalist Church v. Colegrove, 74 Conn. 79.

"It is no doubt true that profits do not of necessity always remain such, and that they may be converted into permanent capital without any formal action or declaration on the part of the corporation or its directors. (Minot v. Paine, 99 Mass. 101.) But they do not become capital by mere accumulation and accretion except in special cases and under special charter provisions, . . . nor by the

Where a corporation had invested earnings in the purchase of its own stock held by a trustee, a distribution of this stock to its shareholders was held to be a dividend of income. (Leland *v.* Hayden, 102 Mass. 542.)

Where a manufacturing corporation had retained a large amount of its earnings, part of which it invested in western lands, in government bonds, and in railroad stocks, it was held that a large cash dividend based upon such floating capital belonged to income. (Matter of Rogers, 161 N. Y. 108; see also Stewart *v.* Phelps, 71 App. Div. 91, 173 N. Y. 621.)

Dividends out of Increases to Working Capital. It is a very common practice for corporations to devote surplus earnings to enlarging and improving the working capital of the concern, without increasing the capital stock. Does the investment of earnings in the working capital of the company permanently capitalize the earnings, so that a subse-

---

mere lapse of time, though that may be the practical effect in cases where in consequence thereof it becomes difficult or impossible to distinguish them from capital. So long as their identity is preserved, we do not see why the directors may not regard them as profits and treat them accordingly. . . . In order to become capital they should be applied, we think, in some effectual way to a permanent increase of the property which is used in the business of the corporation. They may be set aside as matter of bookkeeping for such a use, but until actually appropriated to that purpose they remain, it seems to us, profits, and the corporation and its directors may deal with them as such." Morton, J., in Hemenway *v.* Hemenway, 181 Mass. 406, 410.

quent cash dividend based upon them is a dividend which a trustee must treat as belonging to principal? The opinions bearing on this point are somewhat unsatisfactory, because it is not always made clear just what the courts mean by capital. (Clark & Marshall, Private Corporations, Vol. II, § 375.)

On principle there seems to be no reason for any distinction between an extraordinary dividend based upon earnings which have been simply accumulated, or invested temporarily in securities or in a business which is not the business of the corporation, and a dividend based upon earnings which have been put into the working capital of the corporation but have been withdrawn without impairing the fundamental capital. Directors, except where there are special charter provisions to the contrary, have the right to reconvert into cash earnings thus put into the business, and, provided such temporary capital can still be identified and separated from the fundamental capital, to distribute the proceeds among the shareholders, even where they are forbidden to declare dividends out of capital.

This view has been taken in the case of Smith v. Dana, 60 At. Rep. 117 (Conn., 1905). In that case the Holyoke Water Power Co. had, since the creation of the trust, and about twenty years after it was incorporated, taken up the manufacture and sale of electricity as a side issue, and had built a plant for that purpose. After the company had operated the plant for about twenty years, the city took it by right of eminent domain, paying for it $720,000. The actual cost of the plant to the company had been $245,000. These proceeds were distributed in an extraordinary cash dividend of 65 per cent. The company owned property worth $4,000,000 over and above its liabilities, and its capital stock was $1,200,000. After the dividend the market value of the shares fell from about $380 to about $320. It was held that this dividend was a dividend from income. Although it was not shown, and probably could not have been shown, whether the plant had been built with funds derived from earnings or from the proceeds of new stock, the court took the view that a cash dividend is income unless shown to have been derived from capital. It was reasoned that the doctrine of "once capital always capital" applies only to the fundamental capital which represents the capital stock. "Capital, in that sense, constitutes a fund so set apart and devoted to the corporate uses and the security of creditors that the law jealously guards it from the encroachment of directors in the declaration of dividends. It is placed beyond their reach for that purpose, and no way is open to return it to the share owners. Its dedication is irrevocable, and it must ever remain a fund held in trust for creditors, unless some judicial or other process authorized by legislation intervene. Of it it may well be said "once capital always capital." It is not so of undistributed profits or surplus in any form. They may be effectually dedicated to corporate uses through the processes of a stock dividend, but until so dedicated they are not removed from the reach and control of directors. The manner of utilization may be changed, investments altered, permanent property sold and turned into cash, and experimental or other enterprises abandoned, with a realization upon the investments therein, all at the discretion of directors, with no such artificial consequence that the assets thus employed change their character as the result of the process. Investment in permanent works does not and ought not to capitalize. Directors can, in their discretion, fairly exercised, withhold profits and employ them in the conduct and enlargement of the business. By the same right they ought to be able to, and can, withdraw from any action which will enable the assets thus employed to be returned to their original condition, as funds available for distribution to those to whom they might have been originally divided as dividends. Capital of this kind does not bear the perpetual stamp of capital."

The foregoing case is the only one which has actually decided the point involved, but the language of the other decisions shows it extremely doubtful if the case would be extensively followed. The Supreme Court of Massachusetts, in a dictum, seems of the opinion that profits which are applied " in some effectual way to a permanent increase of the property which is used in the business of the corporation" are thereby permanently capitalized, and the court felt it necessary to distinguish between profits thus capitalized, and profits held as a "floating capital" (Hemenway *v.* Hemenway, 181 Mass. 406, 411). A dictum in the English case of Bouch *v.* Sproule, L. R. 12 App. Cas. 385, 402, by Lord Watson, seems to give some countenance to the rule of the Connecticut decision.

Jurisdictions which apportion extraordinary cash dividends out of accumulated income would probably not distinguish between such a dividend and a dividend from floating capital.

It is possible that the Massachusetts court and those that adhere to the Massachusetts rule will distinguish, on the ground of intention of the creator of the trust, between earnings thus temporarily capitalized before the trust was established, or before the stock was acquired by the trust estate, and earnings temporarily capitalized during the time the stock is held by the trust estate or during the life estate. It is going very far to hold that the creator of a trust or of a life estate could have intended that income should include the proceeds of any considerable part of what was being used as working capital at the time such estate was created.

Dividends in Liquidation. In jurisdictions which hold that it is the declaration of the dividend from income of the corporation which makes it income of the stockholders, a division in liquidation of the property of the corporation without any separation by the corporation of capital from income belongs entirely to principal, even though a large part of the assets consisted of accumulated earnings in the form of floating capital. (Gifford *v.* Thompson, 115 Mass. 478; Second Universalist Church *v.* Colegrove, 74 Conn. 79; In re Armitage, (1893), 3 Ch. 337; see Hemenway *v.* Hemenway, 181 Mass. 406.)

New York Rule. But the courts of New York will in such a case give to income so much of the final dividend as is based upon accumulated earnings which have not been put into the working capital of the corporation. That is, if the directors do not separate income from capital, the court will. (Matter of Rogers, 161 N. Y. 108.) In the last cited case accumulated earnings, which had been put into the working capital, including cash kept on hand to pay the wages of employees and buy new material, were treated as part of the capital.

Rights belong to Principal. Rights given to stockholders to subscribe for new stock at par when the stock is worth more than par belong to the principal of the investment, and if they are sold the proceeds also belong to the principal. Rights, although valuable, are not dividends, and the gain from a sale of rights will usually be exactly balanced by a loss in value of the old shares. (Atkins *v.* Albree, 12 Allen, 359; Moss's Appeal, 83 Pa. St. 264; Biddle's Appeal, 99 Pa. St. 278; Greene *v.* Smith, 17 R. I. 28; Peirce *v.* Burroughs, 58 N. H. 302; Brinley *v.* Grou, 50 Conn. 66; De Koven *v.* Alsop, 205 Ill.

309; Hite's Devisees *v.* Hite's Ex'r, 93 Ky. 257; Eisner's Appeal, 175 Pa. St. 143. But see contra, Wiltbank's Appeal, 64 Pa. St. 256.)

This rule is not inconsistent with the doctrine that stock dividends founded upon earnings belong to income, because, although the rights may be valuable on account of an accumulation of surplus earnings, the issue of the new stock for which the par value is paid does not represent a division of these earnings. The issue of new stock simply increases the number of shares that are entitled at some time to a division of the earnings. (Moss's Appeal, 83 Pa. St. 264.) [1]

Summary. It is apparent from the foregoing statement of the law that when a dividend is paid to a life tenant or to a trustee who has the duty of keeping income separate from corpus, two principal inquiries are necessary. First, Is the dividend paid out of what is income of the corporation, or is it a distribution of what is capital of the corporation? If

---

[1] The Pennsylvania courts seem to have limited this rule to cases where the new stock is of the same company as that of which the trustees hold stock. In Eisner's Appeal, 175 Pa. St. 143, it was held that valuable rights given to stockholders of F. Co. to subscribe to new stock in E. Co. could not impair the value of stock in the F. Co. held by the trustees, and so were income. (But see Thomson's Estate, 153 Pa. St. 332.)

It would seem that Pennsylvania courts, and those which follow the Pennsylvania rule of giving stock dividends to income when based upon earnings made while the principal shares belonged to the trust, ought to inquire whether such rights are earnings or accretions to capital of the principal corporations.

the dividend is found to have been paid out of what the corporation was entitled to treat as income, no further inquiry would usually be necessary in case of a regular dividend. In case of an extraordinary dividend, the form of the second inquiry differs in different jurisdictions. Under the Massachusetts rule the only question would be whether the dividend was in substance a cash dividend or a stock dividend. Under the Pennsylvania rule the inquiry must be, what part of the dividend was earned while the trust has owned the stock or while the stock has belonged to the life estate.

In determining the answer to the first question there is a presumption that the dividend came out of the corporation's earnings, and the officers of a corporation are, especially for the purposes of such a collateral inquiry, allowed great freedom in determining what increase of property should be treated as earnings and what should be treated as accretions to the value of the property, which constitutes fundamental capital. In the case of regular dividends a trustee is safe in relying on the natural presumption that they are being paid out of the corporation's earnings. The vote declaring extraordinary dividends often states their source with some particularity. In such a case the trustee or life tenant must determine for himself whether what it stated to be the source was income of the corporation or part of its principal property.

It has been found convenient in discussing in detail the law bearing on these two questions to reverse somewhat the logical order and to deal with the second question before disposing of the first.

CHAPTER IV.

APPORTIONMENT OF LOSS OR PROFIT.

It is a general principle universally recognized that loss of principal of an investment falls upon the corpus, that loss of income falls upon the life beneficiary, and that each investment stands by itself. It sometimes happens that there is an entire suspension for a time of income upon an investment because of somebody's default, and a subsequent recovery of an amount not sufficient to repay the entire principal and overdue income of the investment. In such a case it may be necessary to apportion the loss between the principal and income.

Apportionment of Loss on Foreclosure of Mortgage. A common case of this sort is where a trustee has invested in an interest-bearing mortgage and has been obliged to foreclose for non-payment of interest. He may be obliged to buy in the property and hold it for some time, not as an investment, but for the purpose of awaiting an advantageous sale, often without any income or with very little above the expense of holding the property, and even then be obliged to sell at a sum insufficient to replace the original investment and the accrued interest. For ex-

subsequent sale, there seems to be no reason for giving any part of the profit to income. It has been held in such a case that the entire profit belongs to principal. (Neel's Estate (No. 2), 207 Pa. St. 446.)

A similar question may arise when a trustee, having lost part of the principal and income of a trust fund by reason of an unwarranted investment, and having been ordered to pay to the new trustee the amount of the loss, is able to pay only part of what is adjudged to be due from him. The deficiency has been apportioned between principal and income in the same manner as in Trenton Trust & Safe Deposit Co. v. Donnelly (Parsons v. Winslow, 16 Mass. 361.)[1]

[1] But see Cook v. Lowry, 95 N. Y. 103, where it was held that in case of devastavit by a trustee, it will be presumed, in absence of evidence to the contrary, that the trustee used up the income first before using the principal, because the depletion of an estate is ordinarily a gradual process 'and begins by misappropriation of that which would be least likely to attract attention. No apportionment of the loss was made. It is doubtful if this case would be followed in other states.

CHAPTER V.

WHEN ENJOYMENT OF INCOME BEGINS.

It is universal law that if an annuity or the use or income of property is given by will to a person for life or until the happening of a contingency such person is entitled to the income from the date of the testator's death unless the will provides otherwise. (Sargent *v.* Sargent, 103 Mass. 297; Ayer *v.* Ayer, 128 Mass. 575; Rev. Laws Mass. (1902), ch. 141, § 24; California Civil Code (1903), §§ 1366, 1368; Weld *v.* Putnam, 70 Maine, 209; Clifford *v.* Davis, 22 Ill. App. 316; Wethered *v.* Safe Dep. & Trust Co., 79 Md. 153; Eichelberger's Estate, 170 Pa. St. 242; Flickwir's Estate, 136 Pa. St. 374.)

Any income which accumulates in the hands of executors before the principal is turned over to trustees should be treated by the trustees as income and be divided among the life tenants. (Cushing *v.* Burrell, 137 Mass. 21; Smith *v.* Fellows, 131 Mass. 20.) And if for any reason the income has meantime been invested, its earnings also belong to the life tenant. (Lovering *v.* Minot, 9 Cush. 151.)

If, however, it appears to have been the testator's intention that the enjoyment of the income should not begin until some time after his death, his intention will, of course, prevail, and income in the meantime will become part of the principal, unless some other provision were made in the will. (Keith v. Copeland, 138 Mass. 303.)

Income in Case of Delayed Conversion. When property comes to a trustee or executor invested in a manner which he cannot properly continue permanently, either because of some direction in the will or deed creating the trust, or because the investment is not a proper investment for a trustee, the property must be turned as soon as possible into authorized investments. Circumstances must often cause considerable delay in such conversion, and the income from the property in the meantime may be very different in amount from what can be realized from the property after it is properly invested. It is settled law that in such a case the persons entitled to income are not entitled to the entire actual income if that is appreciably larger than what the property, permanently invested as directed, would produce, unless it clearly appears to have been the intention of the creator of the trust that the entire actual income should be paid over as income. (Kinmonth v. Brigham, 5 Allen, 270; Westcott v. Nickerson, 120 Mass. 410; Minot v. Thompson, 106 Mass. 583; Mudge v. Parker, 139 Mass. 153; Healey v. Toppan, 45 N. H. 243; Willard's Ex'r v. Willard, 21 At. Rep. 463 (N. J. Ch. 1891).)

The converse of the proposition seems also to be

general law: that is, if the property before conversion produce less income than might reasonably be expected from the authorized investments, the deficiency should be made up out of the proceeds of the property. (Edwards *v.* Edwards, 183 Mass. 581; Underhill, Trusts, Am. Ed., p. 244.)

Method of determining Amount of Income. Whether part of the actual income is given to the corpus or part of the actual corpus is treated as equitable income, the method of apportionment is in substance as follows: Treat the entire net proceeds of the investment in question, including the actual net income from the beginning of the trust to the time of conversion, as the sum total of the principal and income of a fund invested at the date of the beginning of the trust in the authorized investments, allowing a rate of income which the trustee could reasonably have expected from an authorized investment.

To illustrate, suppose trust property retained for a year in a business yielding a net income of $5,000. On conversion into cash the investment yields $50,000. Assuming that the investments authorized by the trust might reasonably have been expected to yield 4 per cent net income, the amount of the $55,000, the entire net proceeds to be retained as principal may be found by dividing $55,000 by $1.04. The result gives $50,961.54 as the permanent principal and $4,038.46 to income, the income being exactly 4 per cent of the permanent principal. If

WHEN ENJOYMENT OF INCOME BEGINS.

the period covered is more than a year, compound interest with annual rests should be allowed to income. For example, in the case supposed, the divisor for a period of two years would be $1.0816. (Westcott v. Nickerson, 120 Mass. 410; Edwards v. Edwards, 183 Mass. 581, 584; Kinmonth v. Brigham, 5 Allen, 270.)

Common situations where this doctrine would be applied are where part of a testator's property comes to a trustee tied up in a partnership venture from which it can not be at once withdrawn (Kinmonth v. Brigham, 5 Allen, 270; Westcott v. Nickerson, 120 Mass. 410; Mudge v. Parker, 139 Mass. 153; Willard's Ex'r v. Willard, 21 At. Rep. 463 (N. J. Ch. 1891)); or in shipping (Healey v. Toppan, 45 N. H. 243; Brown v. Gellatly, L. R. 2 Ch. 751); or in vacant land which produces little or no income. (Edwards v. Edwards, 183 Mass. 581); or in leasehold property (Minot v. Thompson, 106 Mass. 583).[1]

[1] In Edwards v. Edwards, cited above, the trustees, who had been instructed by the will to invest in such securities as the laws of Massachusetts allow savings banks to invest in, and pay the income to testator's widow, held for three years a tract of vacant land, which came to them from the testator and which did not produce enough income to pay taxes. At the time of testator's death the land was appraised at $150,000; the trustees sold it for $196,500. It was held that the net proceeds of the land, after deducting taxes and other expenses, should be apportioned between principal and income. The court ordered the case sent to a master to determine what rate of income the trustees could reasonably have obtained if the property had been invested in securities authorized by the will, declining to allow the legal rate of 6 per cent. The decree finally entered by agreement of parties apportioned the income at the rate of 4 per cent per annum, with annual rests.

Doctrine modified by Testator's Intention. This doctrine is founded upon the presumed intention of the creator of the trust or life estate that income should begin at once, and that income should mean the income of the property in its converted state. When it appears that the creator of the trust intended that until the property was converted the actual income, and that only, should belong to the life beneficiary, of course his intention will control. It is considered a strong indication that the testator intended the entire net profits, or only the actual income of an investment, to be paid to the life tenant, if he has expressly given his trustees power to continue the investment indefinitely at their discretion. (Green *v.* Crapo, 181 Mass. 55; Hite's Devisees *v.* Hite's Ex'r, 93 Ky. 257; Buckingham *v.* Morrison, 136 Ill. 437; Heighe *v.* Littig, 63 Md. 301; Outcalt *v.* Appleby, 36 N. J. Eq. 73; In re Pitcairn, Brandreth *v.* Colvin (1896), 2 Ch. 199.)

In Buckingham *v.* Morrison, 136 Ill. 437, where trustees had been expressly given power by the will to continue to carry on indefinitely any business in which the testator might be engaged, it was held that profits derived from a business carried on by the trustees until an opportunity for conversion constituted income of the trust estate. In Hite's Devisees *v.* Hite's Ex'r, 93 Ky. 257, where trustees, who had been instructed to manage, control, invest, and dispose of the estate " in their discretion, so as to be safe and produce income," held unproductive real estate awaiting a better price, it was decided that only actual income belonged to the life tenant, because the testator must have known that it would be necessary for the trustees to hold part of the land for some time, and there was nothing in the will to indicate that he intended the life tenant to have anything more than actual income.

Disposition of Accumulated Income. Giving property in trust necessarily implies that any income in excess of the sums the trustees are directed to pay out must be accumulated until the division of the estate and added to the sum to be finally divided. Such accumulations become permanently part of the principal. (Brown *v.* Wright, 168 Mass. 506; Minot *v.* Tappan, 127 Mass. 333.) But income which the trustees have the right to hold back temporarily remains income, although retained and accumulated for some time. (Burt *v.* Gill, 89 Md. 145; Williams *v.* Bradley, 3 Allen, 270.)

In cases where trustees are directed to pay to the life tenant so much of the income as may be necessary for his support, or so much as they may deem expedient, and no specific provision is made for disposition of accumulated income, it is a question of interpretation of the testator's intention whether the accumulated income has become part of the principal or is to be distributed to those who are entitled to income. The courts favor a life tenant where he is a near relative and seems to have been the main object of the testator's bounty. (Burt *v.* Gill, 89 Md. 145; Williams *v.* Bradley, 3 Allen, 270.)

CHAPTER VI.

OUTLAY.

A LIFE tenant of property must bear the ordinary expense of keeping the property intact for the remainderman. He must not only not commit waste himself, but must guard against ordinary wear and tear incident to use. (Plympton *v.* Boston Dispensary, 106 Mass. 544.) Similarly a trustee must pay out of income these ordinary expenses of keeping the property up and the expenses of management, unless a different intention has been shown by the creator of the trust. (Cases cited, *infra.*)

Taxes. A life tenant enjoying the income of property must keep it free from incumbrance by paying the ordinary yearly taxes, and a trustee must pay such taxes out of income of the property taxed. (Varney *v.* Stevens, 22 Maine, 331; Cairns *v.* Chabert, 3 Edw. Ch. 312; DeWitt *v.* Cooper, 18 Hun, 67; Peirce *v.* Burroughs, 58 N. H. 302; Bridge *v.* Bridge, 146 Mass. 373; Holmes *v.* Taber, 9 Allen, 246; Dufford *v.* Smith, 46 N. J. Eq. 216; Matter of Tracy, 87 App. Div. (N. Y.) 215, 218; Hagan *v.* Varney, 147 Ill. 281.)

Water Rates. The same is true of water rates. (Bridge *v.* Bridge, 146 Mass. 373.)

Taxes not apportioned as to Time. It has been held that an annual tax assessed on trust property on May first for the year following is payable out of income of a life beneficiary who died before the end of the year, and is not apportionable. (Holmes *v.* Taber, 9 Allen, 246.) But it is evidently the practice in Pennsylvania to apportion the tax in such cases. (Crump's Estate, 13 Pa. Co. Ct. R. 286.)

Taxes assessed on an estate before the death of a testator constitute a debt of his estate, and are payable out of the *corpus* of his estate, even though they are for a period which begins only a few days before his death. (Matter of Babcock, 52 Hun, 142.)

Special Taxes for Permanent Improvements apportioned. Taxes assessed because of betterments in the form of permanent improvements in the locality or in the property itself, such as laying out a new street or putting in a sewer, must be borne by both life tenant and remainderman. In case of a life estate, theoretically such a tax should be paid by the remainderman, and the life tenant should then pay him interest each year on the tax. In practice the matter is adjusted by charging to the life tenant the present worth of an annuity equal to the annual interest running during the number of years which constitute the expectancy of life of the life tenant as figured by the life insurance tables; the balance must be borne by the remainderman. (Moore *v.* Simonson, 27 Or. 117;

Plympton v. Boston Dispensary, 106 Mass. 544; Estate of Miller, 1 Tuck. (N. Y. Sur.) 346.)

Where such a tax is assessed upon a trust estate, the trustee has simply to pay the whole tax out of the principal in which both life tenant and remainderman are interested. (Plympton v. Boston Dispensary, 106 Mass. 544.)

Taxes for Lasting Improvements. Taxes assessed because of lasting improvements, which are likely, however, to wear out during the existence of the life estate, should be paid out of income or by the life tenant. (Hitner v. Ege, 23 Pa. St. 305; Reyburn v. Wallace, 93 Mo. 326.) If the betterments, though not permanent, are likely to last beyond the life of the life tenant, the tax should be equitably apportioned according to the benefit likely to be received by each estate. (Pratt v. Douglas, 38 N. J. Eq. 517, 542; Peck v. Sherwood, 56 N. Y. 615; Fleet v. Dorland, 11 How. Pr. 489; Huston v. Tribbetts, 171 Ill. 547; Bobb v. Wolff, 54 Mo. App. 515; Wordin's Appeal, 71 Conn. 531.)

In Bobb v. Wolff, 54 Mo. App. 515, a special tax was assessed for constructing a granite pavement in front of an estate. The evidence was that the life of such a pavement was ordinarily about twenty-five years. The life tenant was seventy-six years old at the date of the tax bill. His expectation of life by the life insurance tables was 5.88 years. It was held that one quarter of the tax bill should be paid by the life tenant and three quarters by the remainderman.

In Reyburn v. Wallace, 93 Mo. 326, a tax for the same sort of pavement was held chargeable to the life tenant, who was only twenty-eight years old. His expectation of life was over thirty-six years, and, although there was no evidence on the point, the court thought that the pavement could not be expected to last longer than thirty-six years.

A tax assessed for laying out a new street in front of property has been held payable out of principal (Plympton v. Boston Dispensary, 106 Mass. 544), also a tax assessed for laying in a sewer (Tragbar's Estate, 12 Pa. Co. Ct. R. 635), and for connecting a house with a sewer (Bradley's Estate, 3 Pa. Dist. Ct. R. 359). A tax assessed for laying a brick sidewalk (Hitner v. Ege, 23 Pa. St. 305), or an asphalt sidewalk (Wordin's Appeal, 71 Conn. 531), has been held payable from income or by the life tenant.

Taxes upon Unproductive Property. Taxes upon unimproved property which produces no income should be paid out of the *corpus* of the estate. (Stone v. Littlefield, 151 Mass. 485; Clark v. Middlesworth, 82 Ind. 240; Murch v. Smith M'f'g Co., 47 N. J. Eq. 193; In re Martens' Estate, 39 N. Y. S. 189; Patterson v. Johnson, 113 Ill. 559, 576.) It has been held that, although the liability of a tenant for life to pay ordinary taxes is limited to the rental value of the property, rents for the whole term of his estate are answerable for the payment of taxes accruing during said term. (Murch v. Smith M'f'g Co., 47 N. J. Eq. 193.)

Inheritance Taxes. Inheritance taxes upon the interest of a life tenant or life beneficiary are payable out of income. Such a tax upon the interest of the remainderman is payable out of the *corpus*. (Sohier *v.* Eldredge, 103 Mass. 345; Brown's Estate, 208 Pa. St. 161.)

Repairs. A life tenant is required to keep the premises in reasonably good repair. (Clemence *v.* Steere, 1 R. I. 272; Kearney *v.* Ex'r of Kearney, 17 N. J. Eq. 504; Murch *v.* Smith M'f'g Co., 47 N. J. Eq. 193.) He is not obliged to make improvements or additions, and if he does so, although the value of the estate of the remainderman is thereby increased, the life tenant cannot encumber the estate or charge the remainderman with the expense of such improvements. (Caldecott *v.* Brown, 2 Hare 144; Pratt *v.* Douglas, 38 N. J. Eq. 516, 542.)

Alterations and Additions. A trustee must pay for ordinary repairs, such as are made to keep the estate in good condition, out of income. (Little *v.* Little, 161 Mass. 188; Abell *v.* Brady, 79 Md. 94, 101.) But the expense of alterations and additions should be charged to the corpus of a trust fund. (Abell *v.* Brady, 79 Md. 94, 101; In re Parr, 92 N. Y. S. 990.) Thus the cost of changing into stores the lower story of buildings which had been used as dwelling houses is chargeable to principal, as is also the cost of changing an apartment hotel into an office building. But the expense of entirely replumbing a house, repapering, painting, and putting in a new elevator to replace an old one, all at a cost of nearly double the annual rent, has been held chargeable to income. (Little *v.* Little, 161 Mass. 188.)

Repairs of Newly Purchased Property. Expense of putting into tenantable repair property purchased, or otherwise acquired by trustees, is properly chargeable to principal as part of the original investment, though subsequent repairs of that nature would fall upon income. (Parsons *v.* Winslow, 16 Mass. 361.)

Where trustees have power to sell property left by the testator and to reinvest, but choose to retain the property and expend considerable sums in repairs and alterations, it has been held that the cost of these repairs and alterations should be charged to principal as a new investment of trust funds. (Sohier *v.* Eldredge, 103 Mass. 345.) On the other hand it was held by the same court in a later case (Little *v.* Little, 161 Mass. 188) that there is no reason for drawing a line at a testator's death so that repairs then needed should be called improvements and charged to principal. In apportioning expenses in the nature of repairs and improvements between income and principal, a trustee's judgment will probably not be disturbed by the courts except when clearly wrong. (Little *v.* Little, 161 Mass. 188.) The general principle controlling should be that what is designed merely to renew, or repair waste or wearing out should be charged to income, and what is designed permanently to increase the value of the corpus should be charged to principal.

Insurance. A life tenant is not bound to insure the interest of the remainderman, but each may insure his own interest. (Harrison v. Pepper, 166 Mass. 288; DeWitt v. Cooper, 18 Hun, 67.) A trustee who holds the legal title for both has the duty of insuring; and accordingly insurance premiums paid by a trustee would probably be universally treated as an ordinary expense of holding and managing the property, and so payable out of income. (Bridge v. Bridge, 146 Mass. 373.) The general practice of trustees is to charge insurance premiums to income. (Loring's Trustee's Handbook, 2d ed., p. 116.)

Insurance money which comes to a trustee because of either partial or total loss should be used in rebuilding, or reinvested as part of the principal, the income of it only belonging to the life beneficiary. Similarly, in case of insurance money paid to a life tenant, if the insurance was on the property itself, the money is the corpus of the estate in another form, and should either be used in rebuilding or be invested. (Clyburn v. Reynolds, 31 S. C. 91, 119.) If, however, the insurance money represents only the interest of the life tenant, it, of course, belongs entirely to him. (Harrison v. Pepper, 166 Mass. 288.)

Interest on Incumbrances. Interest on an incumbrance on the property, for example a mortgage, must be paid by a life tenant, although it would not be safe for a remainderman as against the mortgagee to rely on the liability of the life tenant to pay the interest. (Martin v. Martin, 146 Mass. 517; Plympton v. Boston Dispensary, 106 Mass. 544.) Similarly, a trustee who places an incumbrance on property, or allows one to remain, should pay the interest out of income. If the trustee pays off the principal of the incumbrance he should pay it out of the principal of the trust fund of which both the life tenant and remainderman are beneficiaries. (Martin v. Martin, 146 Mass. 517; Plympton v. Boston Dispensary, 106 Mass. 544.)

If a remainderman pays off the incumbrance, the life tenant must continue to pay interest to the remainderman, or, what is more usual, must pay to the remainderman the present worth of an annuity equal to the annual interest running during the number of years which constitute the expectancy of life of the tenant for life. (Moore v. Simonson, 27 Or. 117; Plympton v. Boston Dispensary, 106 Mass. 544.)

Expenses of Management. — Trustees' Charges. The expenses of managing a trust estate should come out of current income. (Peirce v. Burroughs, 58 N. H. 302; Butterbaugh's Appeal, 98 Pa. St. 351; Wordin's Appeal, 71 Conn. 531.) Such expenses include trustees' charges for investing the fund and collecting the income, and reasonable sums paid in counsel fees in regard to matters concerning management. (Parker *v.* Ames, 121 Mass. 220 ; Danly *v.* Cummins's Ex'r., 31 N. J. Eq. 208.) It seems that expense of changing investments should also come out of income. (Parker *v.* Hill, 185 Mass. 14.)

Brokerage. Brokerage on changes of investment is paid out of income. (Heard *v.* Eldredge, 109 Mass. 258.) Brokerage on the sale or purchase of real estate is in practice charged to principal, because the custom is to treat such brokerage as part of the price of the property. (Loring's Trustee's Handbook, 2d ed., p. 117.)

Commissions on Collections of Principal. It is the practice of many trustees to make a separate charge against principal for services, in the form of a commission on collections of principal from the sale of rights and from stock dividends, and there is some seeming authority for the practice. (Gordon *v.* West, 8 N. H. 444.) It is extremely doubtful if such collections are substantially different from changes in investments, and the decision of Parker *v.* Hill, 185 Mass. 14, discountenances the practice of distinguishing between such service and other service of management. (See also Spangler's Estate, 21 Pa. St. 335.)

It has been held that the expense of bringing foreclosure suits which proved fruitless was chargeable to income, because properly incident to the management of the trust. (Wordin's Appeal, 71 Conn. 531.)

If a trustee neglects to deduct from current income charges which income should properly bear, he cannot deduct them from other income from the same property payable to a person who is subsequently entitled. (Parker v. Ames, 121 Mass. 220.)

Costs of Bill for Instructions. Costs of all parties in a suit properly brought by a trustee to clear up an ambiguity in the language of the will are payable out of the corpus of the fund or property involved. (Bowditch v. Soltyk, 99 Mass. 136; Deane v. Home for Aged Colored Women, 111 Mass. 132.)

Expenses of Administration. Expenses of managing and carrying out the trust should be carefully distinguished from the expenses of administration of the estate of the testator who created the trust. Expenses of administration, including the expenses of a contest over the probate of a will, are to be taken from corpus (Bartlett, Petitioner, 163 Mass. 509, 522), including also expenses lawfully incurred in defending an estate against claims which accrued in the lifetime of the testator. (Quinn v. Madigan, 65 N. H. 8.)

CHAPTER VII.

APPORTIONMENT OF CURRENT INCOME.

It is a general principle of common law that sums of money payable at fixed times are not to be apportioned when the right to them changes between the times set for payment. The person entitled at the date fixed for payment is entitled to the whole payment. (Dexter *v.* Phillips, 121 Mass. 178; Clapp *v.* Astor, 2 Edw. Ch. 379.)

Rent not apportioned at Common Law. Rent has always been considered as a payment of this sort. The courts refused to take the view that it accrued proportionally from day to day, but viewed each payment of rent as an entirety. Accordingly the common-law rule was that rent was not apportionable between successive owners or between a life tenant and his successor in title. The owner or life tenant at the time the rent period ended was entitled to the whole rent then due. If a life tenant died only one day before a three months' rent period ended, his estate could get none of the rent. (Dexter *v.* Phillips, 121 Mass. 178; Sohier *v.* Eldredge, 103 Mass. 345.)

Since a person entitled to income of trust property has an equitable claim on the income as it comes into the hands of the trustee or as the trustee's right to it accrues, this rule of apportionment affects him. (White v. Stanfield, 146 Mass. 424.) Accordingly under the common-law rule a trustee should pay to the first taker of income which comes to the trustee as rent only such portion of the rent as was due at the time such beneficiary ceased to be entitled to the income. If his right to income ceased in the middle of a rent period, the trustee should not pay to him or his representatives any part of the rent which had accrued but was not due. (Adams v. Adams, 139 Mass. 449.)

Another point of time which is important in the question of apportionment is the date of the testator's death. In the absence of statute, income not apportionable at common law which becomes due after the testator's death must be classed as income, regardless of how long it has been accruing, and will go to persons entitled to income at the time it becomes due. (Dexter v. Phillips, 121 Mass. 178; Matter of Kernochan, 104 N. Y. 618; McKeen's Appeal, 42 Pa. St. 479.)

Statute Law of Apportionment of Rent. This rule, especially as applied to rent for a period which had partly elapsed at the death of a life tenant, seemed so unjust, that many States have enacted statutes changing the rule. Some States have made all income apportionable as between persons successively entitled, as if it accrued from day to day. (Rev. Laws of Mass. (1902) ch. 141, §§ 24, 25; N. Y.

Code of Civil Procedure, § 2720; Matter of Young, 23 Misc. (N. Y.) 223; Miller *v.* Crawford, 26 Abb. N. C. 376: Matter of Franklin, 26 Misc. (N. Y.) 107; Code of N. Car. (1883), § 1748; Gen. Laws R. I. (1896), ch. 203, §§ 38, 39); English Apportionment Act of 1870, 33 & 34 Vict., ch. 35.

Others have enacted simply that rent shall be apportioned to a life tenant up to the time of his death. Under these statutes a trustee holding the fee would be required to apportion to income of a life beneficiary such part of rent as had accrued, though not then payable, at the time of the death of the life beneficiary. (Digest of Stats. of Ark. (1894), § 4453; Laws of Del. (1893), ch. 120, § 15; Rev. Stats. of Ill. (Hurd, 1903), ch. 80, § 35; Burns' Annot. Stats. of Ind. (1901), § 7104; Ind. Terr. Stats. (1899), § 2837; Code of Iowa, Annot. (1897), § 2988; Ky. Stats. (1903), § 3865; Redmond *v.* Bedford, 80 Ky. 13; Annot. Code of Miss. (1892), § 2543; Rev. Stats. of Mo. (1899), § 4098; Gen. Stats. of N. J. (1709–1893), Vol. II, p. 1915, § 2; Brightly's Purdon's Digest of Pa. Stats. (12th ed.), Vol. I, p. 584, §§ 71, 72; Borie *v.* Crissman, 82 Pa. St. 175; Civil Code of S. C. (1902), Vol. I, §§ 2408, 2409; Code of Tenn. (1896), § 4184; Rowan *v.* Riley, 6 Bax. (Tenn.) 67; Va. Code, Annot. (1904), §§ 2809, 2810; Code of W. Va. (4th ed. 1899), ch. 94, § 1, and ch. 95, § 1; Wisc. Stats. (1898), § 2193.)

APPORTIONMENT OF CURRENT INCOME.   73

Annuities not apportioned at Common Law. Annuities belong with rent in the class of sums of money payable on fixed dates, and in general are not apportionable to the death of the annuitant except by statute. (Wiggin v. Swett, 6 Met. 194, 201; Bailey's Estate, 23 Pa. C. C. 139; Heizer v. Heizer, 71 Ind. 526; Henry v. Henderson, 81 Miss. 743; Kearney v. Cruikshank, 117 N. Y. 95; Chase v. Darby, 110 Mich. 314.) An annuity may be defined to mean any fixed sum of money granted or bequeathed payable at regular periods. (Nehls v. Sauer, 119 Iowa, 440; Bates v. Barry, 125 Mass. 83.)

Exceptions. An exception has always been made where the annuity was evidently given for the support of a minor child or of a wife living separate from her husband. Such annuities are apportioned to the date of the annuitant's death. (Quinn v. Madigan, 65 N. H. 8; In re Nathan Cushing's Will, 58 Vt. 393; In re Lackawanna Iron & Coal Co., 37 N. J. Eq. 26; Henry v. Henderson, 81 Miss. 743.) The courts of some States have extended this exception to include all annuities which seem to have been intended for the support of the annuitant. (In re Lackawanna Iron v. Coal Co., 37 N. J Eq. 26; In re Nathan Cushing's Will, 58 Vt. 393; Quinn v. Madigan, 65 N. H. 8; Note to Henry v. Henderson, 63 L. R. A. 616.) Some States have extended the exception to annuities given in lieu of dower, on the ground that, as dower would last to the date of the widow's death, what is given in place of it should last as long. (R. I. Hospital Trust Co. *v.* Harris, 20 R. I. 160; Blight *v.* Blight, 51 Pa. St. 420; Parker *v.* Seeley, 56 N. J. Eq. 110.) Other States have refused to carry the exception as far. (Mower *v.* Sandford, 76 Conn. 504; Chase *v.* Darby, 110 Mich. 314. See note to Henry *v.* Henderson, 63 L. R. A. 616.)

Statute Law of Apportionment of Annuities. Some States have by statute made annuities apportionable up to the death of the annuitant. (R. L. of Mass., ch. 141, § 25; N. Y. Code of Civil Procedure, § 2720; Code of W. Va. (4th ed., 1899), ch. 95, § 1; Va. Code, Annot. (1904), § 2810; Ky. Stats. (1903), § 2070; Code of No. Car. (1883), § 1748. Eng. Apportionment Act of 1870, (33 & 34 Vict. c. 35).) The statutes of Rhode Island contain a similar provision in regard to annuities given by will or by an instrument in the nature thereof. (Gen. Laws R. I. (1896), ch. 203, § 39.)

When no different intention is apparent in the will or other instrument creating an annuity it is taken to be payable yearly on the anniversary of the date of the instrument, or in a case of a will, on the anniversary of the date of the testator's death. (Henry *v.* Henderson, 81 Miss. 743; Kearney *v.* Cruikshank, 117 N. Y. 99; Gibson *v.* Bott, 7 Ves. 89, and note.)

Regular Dividends not apportioned. The regular dividends on shares of stock in corporations or associations based upon current income are not apportionable as to time. Profits made by the company do not belong to the stockholder until a dividend is declared, and until it is declared there is ordinarily no certainty that there will be one. It is moreover impracticable to determine just when within each year profits accrue to the company, for they are not usually a steady accretion. (Clapp *v.* Astor, 2 Edw. Ch. 379; Hyatt *v.* Allen, 56 N. Y. 553; Foote, Appellant, 22 Pick. 299; Greene *v.* Huntington, 73 Conn. 106, 115; Ross's Estate, 2 Kulp. 472; Mann *v.* Anderson, 106 Ga. 818. See contra Ex parte Rutledge, Harp. Eq. (S. C.) 65.)

Effect of Statutes. Even where a statute enacts that "an annuity, or the use, rent, income, or interest of property" shall be apportioned between life tenant and remainderman to the date of the former's death the courts have decided that dividends of corporations are not apportionable. (Granger *v.* Bassett, 98 Mass. 462. See also Adams *v.* Adams, 139 Mass. 449.)

Extraordinary Dividends. The law relating to extraordinary dividends has been dealt with in another place. The question of apportioning extraordinary dividends is a very different one because it is usually possible and even easy in such a case to tell from the annual or semi-annual reports of the company just when the profits of the company accrued, reckoning in periods of a year or six months, or whatever periods are covered by the reports. (Cases cited, supra, p. 24.)

Profits not apportioned. It has also been decided on the same reasoning that where a life beneficiary who is entitled to the profits of the testator's share in a partnership dies between the days of accounting, the profits are not apportionable. The reason is that in business profits do not accrue steadily from day to day and so are incapable of apportionment. (Browne *v.* Collins, L. R. 12 Eq. 586; Jones *v.* Ogle, L. R. 8 Chan. 192; McKeen's Appeal, 42 Pa. St. 479.) In the case of profits of a partnership the important date is not the date on which the profits are ascertained, but the period for which they are ascertained. For example, profits of a partnership for a period of accounting ending May 1st would belong to the person entitled to income on that date although the profits were not ascertained until several months after his interest ceased. (Browne *v.* Collins, L. R. 12 Eq. 586; Jones *v.* Ogle, L. R. 8 Chan. 192.)[1]

Dividends payable after Death of Life Tenant. In case of a dividend, declared by a corporation during the life of the life tenant, but payable on a date before which he dies, the entire dividend belongs to the life tenant. (Hill *v.* Newichawanick Co., 8 Hun, 459, 71 N. Y. 593.) It has also been held in Massachusetts that where, on June 23rd, the corpo-

---

[1] It has been held that profits of partnerships are not apportionable under the English Apportionment Act of 1870, although regular dividends of corporations are apportioned as if the earnings accrued from day to day. (Browne *v.* Collins, L. R. 12 Eq. 586.)

APPORTIONMENT OF CURRENT INCOME. 77

ration declared a dividend, stating that it was out of the gain and profit earned and acquired during the year preceding the 31st day of May, this dividend belongs to the estate of a life tenant who died June 12th. (Johnson *v.* Bridgewater, etc., Co., 14 Gray, 274.) This case seems inconsistent with the accepted doctrine in Massachusetts that profits are not income of the stockholder until the dividend is declared. (See Bates *v.* Mackinley, 31 Beav. 280, contra.)

Dividends by Savings Banks. Semi-annual dividends paid depositors in savings banks, though often spoken of as interest on the deposits, are in the class of dividends of corporations, and as such are not apportionable. (Greene *v.* Huntington, 73 Conn. 106, 114.)

A trustee who sells shares of stock shortly before the time for the declaration of the regular dividend cannot give part of what he receives to income, although he receives a better price for the stock because of the nearness of the dividend day. (Bulkeley *v.* Stephens, L. R. (1896), 2 Ch. 241.)[1]

Interest apportioned. Interest on debts and loans

---

[1] But see Lord Londesborough *v.* Somerville, 19 Beav. 295, where a trustee sold consols a month before the regular dividend day. It was held that the life tenant was entitled to such portion of the selling price as the latter was augmented by the proximity of the dividend. A sufficient reason for this decision may be found in the fact that the dividends on consols are absolutely certain, both as to amount and date of payment, so that it is possible to figure out how much has accrued at any date.

is apportionable at common law. It is considered as accruing from day to day for delay of payment of what is due. (Dexter *v.* Phillips, 121 Mass. 178; Riggs *v.* Cragg, 26 Hun, 89, 98.)

Interest on Mortgage Notes. This is true of interest on mortgage notes where the interest is by contract made payable at certain definite times. The reason given for taking such payments out of the ordinary rule of payments of money coming due at fixed times is that the note or mortgage is only security for the debt and interest. (Dexter *v.* Phillips, 121 Mass. 178; Banner *v.* Lowe, 13 Ves. 135.)

Interest on Consols, etc. The English courts distinguished between interest on debts or notes and interest on the public funds, holding that the latter was by common law not apportionable. It was held to come within the class of payments coming due at fixed times. (Pearly *v.* Smith, 3 Atk. 260; Wilson *v.* Harman, 2 Ves. Sen. 671. See also Warden *v.* Ashburner, 2 De G. & Sm. 366.)

Interest Coupons. The Massachusetts courts have followed the English rule as to interest on the public debt, except in cases coming within the Massachusetts statute of apportionment, and have applied it to interest on coupon bonds of all kinds, including those of private corporations. The reason given for the distinction between such interest and interest on debts is that each interest coupon constitutes a separate contract to pay a definite amount of money at a certain time. They may be separately negotiated, and the owner of a coupon may at maturity sue for the amount, although he is not the holder of the bond. The statute of limitations begins to run on each coupon at its maturity. When coupons have been separated from the bond to which they were originally attached, they are not affected by a cancellation or payment of the bond. For these reasons it was held in Massachusetts that each coupon represented an obligation distinct from the bond and from each other coupon, and could not by any fiction be taken as representing interest on the bonds accruing from day to day. (Dexter *v.* Phillips, 121 Mass. 178.)

The Pennsylvania and New York courts seem to have taken a different view, and would probably apportion interest on coupon bonds. (Wilson's Appeal, 108 Pa. St. 344, overruling Earp's Will, 1 Pars. Eq. 453; U. S. Trust Co. *v.* Tobias, 21 Abb. N. C. 393.)

CHAPTER VIII.

A SUMMARY OF THE STATUTES AND DECISIONS IN THE VARIOUS STATES BEARING UPON APPORTIONMENT OF CURRENT INCOME.

ARKANSAS. If a life tenant who has underlet premises dies before the rent shall become payable, his estate is entitled to such proportion of the rent as shall have accrued before his death. (Digest of Stats. of Ark. (1894), § 4453.)

CONNECTICUT. No statute on apportionment of income.

The decisions hold that there is no apportionment of rent, of annuities, of annuities in lieu of dower, or of dividends, including dividends to depositors in savings banks. Interest payable semi-annually is apportionable. (Greene *v.* Huntington, 73 Conn. 106, 114; Mower *v.* Sanford, 76 Conn. 504.)

Tenant for life is entitled to a crop sowed before his death but harvested after his death. (Bradley *v.* Bailey, 56 Conn. 374.)

DELAWARE. If a life tenant who has underlet premises dies before the rent shall become payable, his estate is entitled to such proportion of the rent as shall have accrued before his death. (Laws of Del. (1893), ch. 120, § 15.)

GEORGIA. Life tenant or his legal representatives are entitled to profits of crop sowed by him although his estate be terminated, not by his act, before harvest, whether the crop be annual or perennial. (Code of Ga. (1895), Vol. II, § 3092.) The Code also enacts that if a tenant for life rents the land for a year, and dies, or the estate is otherwise terminated during the year, the tenant shall be entitled to the land for the term of the year, upon complying with his contract with the life tenant. (§ 3093.)

ILLINOIS. Statutes give to executors or administrators of a life tenant of lands, who has died before the day when any rent shall become due from an under-tenant, the right to recover from the latter the proportion of rent which accrued before the death of the life tenant. (Rev. Stats. of Ill. (Hurd–1903), chap. 80, § 35.)

INDIANA. Executor or administrator of a life tenant who dies before the day when any rent is to become due may recover from the under-tenant the proportion of rent which accrued before his death, and the remainderman shall recover the residue. (Burns' Annot. Stats. of Ind. (1901), § 7104.)

INDIAN TERRITORY. Statutes (1899), § 2837, provide for apportionment of rent to life tenant up to the time of his death.

IOWA. The executor of a tenant for life who dies before rent is payable and a person entitled to rent dependent on the life of another may recover from the under-tenant the proportion of the rent which had accrued at the time of the death. (Code of Iowa, Annot. (1897), § 2988.)

Annuities are not apportionable except in the recognized exceptions. (Nehls *v.* Sauer, 119 Iowa, 440.)

KENTUCKY. Statutes enact that "when a person who has a freehold or an uncertain interest in land" rents the land and dies before the rent shall have become due, the rent "shall be apportioned between the personal representatives of the deceased and the person who shall succeed to the land as heir, personal representative, devisee, or person in reversion or remainder, unless in the case of a devisee the will shall otherwise direct." (Ky. Stats. (1903), § 3865.) This statute applies to life tenant and remainderman. (Redmon *v.* Bedford, 80 Ky. 13.)

Emblements of lands of a person dying after March 1st, which shall be severed before December 31st following, belong to his personal representatives. (Ky. Stats. (1903), § 3862.)

Annuities are also apportioned to the death of the annuitant in proportion to the time elapsed. (Ky. Stats. (1903), § 2070.)

MASSACHUSETTS. Statute enacts that a person entitled by will, deed, or other instrument, to an annuity or the rent, income, or interest of property for life or until the happening of a contingency, or his representative, shall have the same apportioned if his right or estate therein terminates between the days on which it is payable, unless otherwise provided in the will or instrument. (Rev. Laws of Mass. (1902), ch. 141, § 25.) It is important to notice that the statute applies only to cases where the limited estate is created by will or other instrument, and so would not apply where a widow or husband acquires a life estate under statute. Moreover the statute applies only as between life tenants, or life beneficiaries, or persons whose estate or enjoyment of income is to terminate on the happening of some contingency and the persons entitled next after them. It applies only at the termination of such limited estate and so has no application to apportionment on changes of investment. Sargent v. Sargent, 103 Mass. 297.

In cases where the statute applies the following kinds of income are apportionable as to time: interest on notes or debts (White v. Stanfield, 146 Mass. 424); interest on coupon bonds (Adams v. Adams, 139 Mass. 449); rent and annuities. Dividends on shares of stock are not apportionable even under the statute, and probably not profits of a business. (Granger v. Bassett, 98 Mass. 462.)

In cases which do not come within the statute the common-law rules apply. In such cases interest on money loaned on mortgage notes is apportionable

(Foote, Appellant, 22 Pick. 299), but interest on coupon bonds is not apportionable except in cases which come within the application of the statute. A semi-annual interest coupon falling due a week after a testator's death would all belong to income, but semi-annual interest on a mortgage note falling due at the same time would be apportioned between principal and income. (Dexter *v.* Phillips, 121 Mass. 178; Sargent *v.* Sargent, 103 Mass. 297.) Rent is not apportionable except by the statute. (Dexter *v.* Phillips, 121 Mass. 178.)

Where a trustee sells coupon-bearing bonds between the interest days, no separate sum being charged for accrued interest, although the accrued interest would increase the price of the bonds, none of the money received is set apart to the persons entitled to income. (Sargent *v.* Sargent, 103 Mass. 297.) But when, as is customary in the Boston market on a purchase or sale of bonds, a separate charge is made for " accrued interest," this accrued interest should be charged to income on a purchase by a trustee and given to income on a sale. (Hemenway *v.* Hemenway, 134 Mass. 446.)

MICHIGAN. No statute on apportionment of income. Annuities are not apportionable except when given to a married woman living separate from her husband, or for the maintenance of a minor. (Chase *v.* Darby, 110 Mich. 314.)

MISSISSIPPI. Statute enacts that tenant for life or for life of another shall have rent apportioned to time of death or ceasing of his estate. (Annot. Code of Miss. (1892), § 2543.)

MISSOURI. Similar statute to that in Mississippi. (Rev. Stats. Mo. (1899), § 4098.)

NEW HAMPSHIRE. No statute on apportionment. Common-law rules of apportionment of rent, annuities, interest, and dividends prevail. (Quinn *v.* Madigan, 65 N. H. 8. But see Perry *v.* Aldrich, 13 N. H. 343.)

Annuities to widow in lieu of dower are apportioned. (Quinn *v.* Madigan, 65 N. H. 8.)

NEW JERSEY. By statute a life tenant is entitled to a proportional part of rent up to the date of his death, although the rent is not then due and the rent period has not expired. (General Statutes of N. J. (1709-1895), Vol. II, p. 1915.)

An annuity to a wife evidently given for her support is apportioned to the date of her death. (In re Lackawanna Iron & Coal Co., 37 N. J. Eq. 26.) An annuity in lieu of dower is also apportioned. (Parker *v.* Seeley, 56 N. J. Eq. 110.)

NEW YORK. Statutes require apportionment of rents, annuities, dividends, and other payments of every description made payable or becoming due at fixed periods under any instrument executed after June 7, 1875, or any will taking effect after that date, so that on the death of any person interested in such rents, annuities, etc., or in the estate or fund from or in respect to which they are derived, or on the determination by any other means of his interest, he or his representatives shall be entitled to a proportion of such rents, etc., according to the time which has elapsed since the last payment was due. (Code of Civil Procedure, N. Y., § 2720.)

Under the statute, income of trust estates, except dividends on shares of stock, is apportioned to the death of the life tenant. (Matter of Young, 23 Misc. (N. Y.) 223.)

The statute does not provide for apportionment of income to the date of the death of a testator who creates the life estate or the trust. (Miller v. Crawford, 26 Abb. N. C. 376; Matter of Franklin, 26 Misc. 107; Matter of Weeks, 5 Dem. 194.) In cases which do not come within the statute rent is not apportioned as to time (Marshall v. Moseley, 21 N. Y. 280), nor are annuities except annuities for support (Clapp v. Astor, 2 Edw. Ch. 379). Interest on money lent is apportionable without the aid of the statute. (Clapp v. Astor, 2 Edw. Ch. 379; Riggs v. Cragg, 26 Hun, 89, 98.) Dividends on shares of stock are not apportionable. (Matter of Kane, 64 App. Div. 566; Hyatt v. Allen, 56 N. Y. 553; Matter of Kernochan, 104 N. Y. 618; Clapp v. Astor, 2 Edw. Ch. 379.) Dividends declared before a testator's death, but payable after, belong to the principal of the estate. (Matter of Kernochan, 104 N. Y. 618; Hill v. Newichawanick Co., 8 Hun, 459, 71 N. Y. 593.) Income derived from bonds and mortgages and from U. S., state, and city bonds is apportionable as accruing from day to day, without the aid of statute. (U. S. Trust Co. *v.* Tobias, 21 Abb. N. C. 392.)

NORTH CAROLINA. The statutes apportion "rents, rent charges, annuities, pensions, dividends, or any other payments of any description" . . . "made payable at fixed periods to successive owners under any instrument or by any will and where the right of any owner to receive payment is terminable by a death or other uncertain event." (Code of No. Car. (1883), § 1748.)

OHIO. No statute. Rents are not apportionable, but a life tenant is entitled to the crop sowed during her life although her estate ceased before the harvest. (Noble *v.* Tyler, 61 O. St. 432.)

PENNSYLVANIA. Statute gives to the executor or administrator of a tenant for life, who dies before rent becomes payable, an action to recover from the under-tenant a proportion of the rent according to the time elapsed at the death of the tenant for life. (Brightly's Purdon's Digest Pa. Stats. (12th ed.), Vol. I, p. 595, § 128. See also p. 584, § 71.) Under this statute a trustee would probably be required to apportion income in the form of rent, at the time of the ceasing of one estate.

Annuities are not apportionable except when for support or in lieu of dower. (Bailey's Estate, 23 Pa.

C. C. 139; Blight *v.* Blight. 51 Pa. St. 420; Gheen *v.* Osborn, 17 Serg. & R. 171.)

Ordinary yearly dividends on shares of stock in a corporation are not apportionable as to time. (Ross' Estate, 2 Kulp, 472.) The same is true of dividends or divisions of profits on a partnership interest in a business continued after the testator's death. (McKeen's Appeal, 42 Pa. St. 479.)

Extraordinary dividends are apportioned. See supra, p. 23.

RHODE ISLAND. Statute enacts that annuities or the use, rent, income, or interest of property given by will or by an instrument in the nature thereof, to or in trust for the benefit of a person for life or until the happening of a contingent event, shall be apportioned to the time of the death of the life tenant or the happening of the contingency. (General Laws of R. I. (1896), ch. 203, §§ 38, 39.)

It will be noticed that, like the Massachusetts statute, it does not change the common-law rule at the death of a testator or on a change of investments.

SOUTH CAROLINA. Statute enacts that rent shall be apportioned in favor of a life tenant up to the time of his death. (Civil Code of S. C. (1902), Vol. I, §§ 2408, 2409.) But the common-law rule remains in force as to rent not due at the time of a testator's death: it all goes to the heir or devisee. (Huff *v.* Latimer, 33 S. C. 255.)

TENNESSEE. Statutes provide for apportionment of rent in favor of a life tenant up to the time of his death. (Code of Tenn. (1896), § 4184.)

The common-law rule against apportionment applies as between heir and administrator on the death of the owner in fee. (Rowan *v.* Riley, 6 Bax. 67.)

VIRGINIA. The statute enacts that on the determination by death or otherwise, of the estate or other thing, from or in respect of which any rent, hire, or money coming due at fixed periods, issues or is derived, or on the death of any person interested therein, the personal representative or assignee of the person who would have been entitled to such rent, hire, or money when it became due, but for such death or determination, shall have a proportion thereof according to the proportion of the time elapsed. (Va. Code, Annot. (1904), §§ 2809, 2810.)

WEST VIRGINIA. The code of West Virginia (4th ed., 1899), ch. 95, contains exactly the same provisions.

WISCONSIN. By statute rent is apportioned to tenant for life up to the date of his death. (Wis. Stats. (1898), § 2193.)

INDEX.

INDEX.

A.

PAGES

ACCUMULATED INCOME,
   added to principal, when 59
   intention of testator as to 59
   in hands of executor before trustee gets the estate,
      remains income 54
   earnings of, are income 54

ADMINISTRATION,
   expenses of, paid from principal 69

ALTERATIONS AND ADDITIONS,
   cost of, in trust property paid by principal . . . 64
   life tenant cannot charge, to remainderman . . 64

ANNUITIES,
   definition of 73
   enjoyment of, begins at death of testator . . . 54
   payable, when 74
   not generally apportioned by common law . . . 73
   for support, apportioned 73
   in lieu of dower, sometimes apportioned . . . 73
   apportionment of, by statute 74

APPORTIONMENT,
   of extraordinary cash dividends, between income
      and principal 21–25, 75
      Massachusetts rule against 22
      Pennsylvania rule in favor of 23
      of stock dividends 28–30

APPORTIONMENT — *Continued.*

method of	29
of loss, between income and principal	50–53
on foreclosure of mortgage	50–53
due to devastavit	53
of profit, between income and principal	52
of current income as to time	70–89
important dates	70–71
annuities	73–74
dividends	74–75
interest on debts and loans	77
mortgage notes	78
public securities	78
coupon bonds	70–79
profits of business	76
rent	70–72

B.

BONDS,

bought at premium, a wasting investment	13
premium on, sometimes replaced out of interest	13–16
profit on sale of, at increased premium, principal	16
interest on, apportionment as to time	78–79
BOTES	7

BROKERAGE,

on changes of investment, payable from income	68
on sale or purchase of real estate, payable from principal	68

C.

CAPITAL,

meaning of word	34–35
fundamental	34
working	35
floating	35

See PRINCIPAL.

INDEX.

COMMISSIONS,
    trustee's, on collections of principal, payable from income 68
CORPUS,
                See PRINCIPAL.
COSTS,
                See EXPENSES.
COUPONS OF INTEREST ON BONDS,
    apportioned as to time in some states 79
    not apportioned in other states 78–79

D.

DIVIDENDS OF CORPORATIONS,
    discretion of officers when to declare 17
    presumed to be from earnings 18
    earnings of corporation not income of stockholder until declaration of dividend 17
    out of fundamental capital belong to principal 17, 35
    out of proceeds of capital not needed in the business 36
    out of proceeds of property taken by right of eminent domain 35
    by land companies, out of proceeds of property sold 38–39
    from proceeds of capitalized earnings 39
    from proceeds of working capital 41–45
    from floating capital, are income 39–41
    in liquidation without separation of earnings . 45–46
  regular dividends:
      not apportioned as to time 19, 74, 75
      effect of apportionment statutes 75
      to depositors in saving banks, not apportioned . 77
      trustees may safely treat, as paid from earnings 18
      if wasting capital, are not wholly income . . 19
      intention of creator of estate as to, when wasting 19

INDEX.

DIVIDENDS OF CORPORATIONS — *Continued*.

  belong to owner of stock at time declared . . 24
  declared before death of life tenant, payable to
   his estate 76
 extraordinary cash dividends 20–25
  not usually based upon current earnings . . . 20
  effect of payment of, on value of stock . . 21–22
  double nature of 20
  Massachusetts rule gives, to income 22
  Pennsylvania rule apportions, according to time
   of accumulation 23–24
  criticisms of both rules 24–25
  different from delayed dividends 33
 stock dividends 25–31
  nature of 25
  not distributions of tangible property . . . 26–27
  do not increase value of holdings 26–27
  declaration of, signifies capitalization of earnings 28
  Massachusetts rule as to 26–27
  New York rule as to 30–31
  Pennsylvania rule as to 28–30
  method of apportionment under Pennsylvania
   rule. 29
 option to take either cash or new stock:
  treated as cash dividend 31
  except where option is only apparent 32
 in form of old shares in which corporation has invested earnings, similar to cash 33, 41
 in form of bonds issued by corporation, similar to
  stock dividend 33
 summary of law as to dividends 47–49
 different from rights 46–47

E.

EARNINGS OF CORPORATIONS,
 not income of stockholder until declaration of dividend. 17, 23

INDEX. 97

PAGE

EARNINGS OF CORPORATIONS — *Continued.*
    accumulated, effect of on value of stock 20
                    interest of stockholder in 20
    made basis of new issue of stock, become capital 39
    added to working capital, effect of 41–45
        See DIVIDENDS and INCOME.

ENJOYMENT OF INCOME,
    begins when 54

ESTOVERS 7

EXPENSES,
    payable from income:
        for maintaining property 60
        for management of trust estate or life estate 60, 67
    payable from principal:
        of suit for interpretation of will 69
        of bill for instructions 69
        of administration 69
        of contest over will 69
        of defending estate from claims against testator 69
    See ALTERATIONS AND ADDITIONS, INCUMBRANCE,
        INSURANCE, REPAIRS, TAXES, WATER RATES.

F.

FIREWOOD,
    right of life tenant to cut 7

FORECLOSURE OF MORTGAGE,
    loss on, apportioned 50–53
    profit on,   "   52
    expense of 68

I.

INCOME,
    definition of 1
    distinguished from increase 1, 38
                    profit 38
    real, distinguished from apparent 1, 38
    must not consume principal 4
    of mines, quarries, and oil wells 5–7

INCOME — *Continued.*

 of timber land 7–13
 of corporation, distinguished from income of stockholder 17
     interest of stockholder in . . . 20
     accumulated, effect on value of
      stock 20
       double nature of . . 20
 of corporation, discretion of directors as to disposition of 25
     accumulated, stockholder has equi-
      table rights in 28
 does not include increase in value of stock due to
  proximity of dividend 77
 accumulated in hands of executor, remains income 54
 in excess of what trustee is directed to pay out,
  becomes principal 59
 temporarily withheld from beneficiary, remains income 59
 enjoyment of, begins when 54–59
 equitable, in case of delayed conversion 55
    how determined 56–57
 from shipping 57
  partnership 57
  leasehold 57
  vacant land 57
 when testator presumed to mean equitable . . . 58
 charges against 60–68
  expenses of management 60, 67
  ordinary taxes 60
  water rates 60
  taxes for lasting improvements, when 62
  ordinary repairs 64
  insurance 66
  interest on incumbrances 66–67
  trustee's charges for services 67
  brokerage on changes of investments, except
   purchase or sale of real estate 68
  trustee's commissions for collecting principal . 68

INDEX. 99

	PAGE

INCOME — *Continued.*
    apportionment of, *see* APPORTIONMENT . . . 70–89
        See DIVIDENDS.
INCREASE,
    in value of principal, belongs to principal . . . 2
    distinguished from income 1, 38
    of premiums on bonds belongs to principal . . 13, 16
INCUMBRANCES,
    interest on, payable from income of trust . . . 67
                     by life tenant 67
    principal of, payable from principal of trust . . 67
                   when paid by remainderman . . . 67
INHERITANCE TAX,
    payable from estate or interest taxed 63
INSURANCE,
    life tenant not obliged to take out 66
    expense of, charged to income of trust 66
    money belongs to principal 66
INTEREST,
    on incumbrances, payable from income of trust 66, 67
                   by life tenant . . 66, 67
    dividends to depositors in savings banks are not 77
    apportionment of 77–79
INVESTMENTS,
    expense of making, payable from income . . . 67
             changing, " " " 68
    For WASTING INVESTMENTS *see* TABLE OF CONTENTS.

L.

LEASEHOLD ESTATES,
    are wasting investments 5
    rent of, belongs partly to principal 5
    equitable income of 57
LIFE TENANT,
    must distinguish carefully between income and
        principal 3

LIFE TENANT — *Continued*.

	PAGE
must repair waste of principal	4
must pay ordinary taxes	60
must keep property in repair	64
cannot charge improvements to remainderman	64
not bound to insure	66
must pay interest on incumbrances	66–67
right of, to dividends. *See* DIVIDENDS.	
income of. *See* INCOME, APPORTIONMENT, WASTING INVESTMENTS.	

LOSS,

of income, not made up out of principal	50
of principal, not made up out of income	50
on foreclosure of mortgage, apportioned	50–51
on devastavit, apportioned	53

M.

MANAGEMENT OF TRUST PROPERTY,

expense of, payable from current income	67

MERGERS,

dividends in cases of	36–38

MINES, QUARRIES, OIL WELLS,

are wasting investments	5
product of, not real income	5
rent or royalties of, how disposed of	5
"open" mines, what are	5
"open" mines, product of, given to income	5–7
intention of creator of estate as to	6

O.

OIL WELLS,

wasting investments	5
See MINES.	

OUTLAY,

See TABLE OF CONTENTS.

P.

PREMIUM, ON BONDS,
    how paid 13
    sinking fund to replace loss of 13–15
    increase of, belongs to principal 13, 16

PRINCIPAL,
    definition of 1, 2
    income must not consume 4
    mere decrease in value of, not to be made up
        out of income 4
    rent from leasehold estates belongs partly to . . 5
    product of mines, quarries, and oil wells, when
        belongs to 5–7
    rent or royalties from mines, quarries, and oil wells,
        when belongs to 5–7
    timber, when belongs to 7–13
    premiums paid from, on bonds should be replaced
        when 13
    sinking fund to replace premiums belongs to, as
        fast as accumulated 13
    profit realized on sale of bonds belongs to . . . 16
    dividends. *See* DIVIDENDS.
    loss of, not to be made up from income 50
    loss on foreclosure of mortgage apportioned . 51–52
    profit on foreclosure of mortgage apportioned . . 52
    loss on devastavit apportioned 53
    excess of real income over equitable, belongs to . 55
    accumulated income not otherwise disposed of
        belongs to 59
    chargeable with taxes assessed before beginning
            of trust or life estate . 61
            for permanent improve-
              ments 62
            equitable part of taxes for last-
              ing improvements 62
            tax upon unproductive prop-
              erty 63

PRINCIPAL — *Continued.*

    chargeable with inheritance tax upon interest of
remainderman 63–64
        alterations and additions . . . 64
        repairs on newly purchased property 65
        extensive repairs on property which trustees have power to sell 65
        expense of permanent improvements 65
        principal of incumbrance . . 67
        brokerage on sale or purchase of real estate 68
        costs and expense of suit for interpretation of will or trust . 69
        expense of administration . . 69
        expense of suits against estate of testator 69
        expense of suits contesting will . 69

PRODUCTS,

    of soil, are ordinarily income 7
    of woodland. *See* TIMBER.
    of mines, quarries, and oil wells, are not real income 5–7

PROFITS,

    not synonymous with income 1, 38
    on sale of bonds, belong to principal 16
    on sale or exchange of stocks, belong to principal 36–38
    on foreclosure of mortgage, apportioned . . . 52
    of business, not apportioned between days of accounting 76
    of business, in case of delayed conversion, not always given to income 56
        See INCOME and INCREASE.

Q.

QUARRIES,
    wasting investments 5
              See MINES.

R.

RENT,
    of leasehold property, not wholly income . . . 5
    of mines, quarries, and oil wells, not income . . 5–7
    not apportioned as to time by common law . . 70–71
    apportionment of, by statutes 71–72
REPAIRS,
    ordinary, must be made by life tenant 64
            charged to income of trust estate . . . 64
    in nature of additions and alterations, charged to
        principal 64
    on newly purchased property, charged to principal 65
    extensive, at beginning of trust estate 65
RIGHTS,
    are not dividends 46–47
    belong to principal 46
ROYALTIES,
    from mines, quarries, and oil wells are not income 5–7

S.

SAVINGS BANKS,
    dividends of, to depositors not apportioned . . 77

T.

TAXES,
    ordinary, payable from income of trust estate . 60
                by life tenant 60
    not apportioned as to time 61
    assessed before death of testator, are debt of estate 61
    for permanent improvements, payable from principal of trust 62

INDEX.

TAXES — *Continued.*
    for permanent improvements, apportioned between
        life tenant and remainderman 61
    for lasting improvements, apportioned . . . 62–63
    upon unproductive property, payable from principal 63
    inheritance, payable from estate taxed 63

TIMBER,
    not wholly income of life tenant 2, 7
    right of life tenant to cut, for firewood and repair
        of fences or buildings 7
    English law as to cutting for profit 8–9
    American law as to cutting for profit 9–13
    proceeds of, when blown down 11

TREES. *See* **TIMBER.**

TRUSTEE,
    duty of, to distinguish between real income and
        principal 1, 3
    duty of, to prevent waste of principal by apparent
        income 4
    duty of, to provide for repairs out of woodland . 7
    charges for services of, payable from income . . 67
        See **INCOME AND PRINCIPAL.**

U.

UNPRODUCTIVE PROPERTY,
    equitable income of, when conversion delayed . . 55
    taxes upon, payable from principal 63

W.

WATER RATES,
    life tenant must pay 60
    payable from income of trust estate 60

WASTING INVESTMENTS 4–16
        See **TABLE OF CONTENTS.**

WOOD AND WOODLAND.
        See **TIMBER.**

Trieste

Trieste Publishing has a massive catalogue of classic book titles. Our aim is to provide readers with the highest quality reproductions of fiction and non-fiction literature that has stood the test of time. The many thousands of books in our collection have been sourced from libraries and private collections around the world.

The titles that Trieste Publishing has chosen to be part of the collection have been scanned to simulate the original. Our readers see the books the same way that their first readers did decades or a hundred or more years ago. Books from that period are often spoiled by imperfections that did not exist in the original. Imperfections could be in the form of blurred text, photographs, or missing pages. It is highly unlikely that this would occur with one of our books. Our extensive quality control ensures that the readers of Trieste Publishing's books will be delighted with their purchase. Our staff has thoroughly reviewed every page of all the books in the collection, repairing, or if necessary, rejecting titles that are not of the highest quality. This process ensures that the reader of one of Trieste Publishing's titles receives a volume that faithfully reproduces the original, and to the maximum degree possible, gives them the experience of owning the original work.

We pride ourselves on not only creating a pathway to an extensive reservoir of books of the finest quality, but also providing value to every one of our readers. Generally, Trieste books are purchased singly - on demand, however they may also be purchased in bulk. Readers interested in bulk purchases are invited to contact us directly to enquire about our tailored bulk rates. Email: customerservice@triestepublishing.com

You May Also Like

The American Law Relating to Income and Principal

Edwin A. Howes

ISBN: 9780649491797
Paperback: 139 pages
Dimensions: 6.14 x 0.30 x 9.21 inches
Language: eng

Building by a builder; practical and economical considerations for the man about to build

Benjamin A. Howes

ISBN: 9780649283200
Paperback: 260 pages
Dimensions: 6.14 x 0.55 x 9.21 inches
Language: eng

www.triestepublishing.com

You May Also Like

Hymnal: For Use in the Services of the Church

Anonymous

ISBN: 9781760579562
Paperback: 178 pages
Dimensions: 5.83 x 0.38 x 8.27 inches
Language: eng

Poems. Lyrical and Dramatic

W. G. Hole

ISBN: 9780649540167
Paperback: 130 pages
Dimensions: 6.14 x 0.28 x 9.21 inches
Language: eng

www.triestepublishing.com

You May Also Like

Shut Your Mouth and Save Your Life

George Catlin

ISBN: 9781760570491
Paperback: 118 pages
Dimensions: 6.14 x 0.25 x 9.21 inches
Language: eng

The Epistle to Diognetus

L. B. Radford

ISBN: 9781760570934
Paperback: 106 pages
Dimensions: 6.14 x 0.22 x 9.21 inches
Language: eng

www.triestepublishing.com

You May Also Like

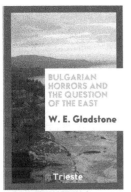

Bulgarian horrors and the question of the East

W. E. Gladstone

ISBN: 9781760571146
Paperback: 46 pages
Dimensions: 6.14 x 0.09 x 9.21 inches
Language: eng

Snow-bound: A Winter Idyl

John Greenleaf Whittier

ISBN: 9781760571528
Paperback: 64 pages
Dimensions: 5.5 x 0.13 x 8.25 inches
Language: eng

Find more of our titles on our website. We have a selection of thousands of titles that will interest you. Please visit

www.triestepublishing.com

Printed in the USA
CPSIA information can be obtained
at www.ICGtesting.com
JSHW012031301023
51146JS00021B/195